THE ADOLESCENT & YOUNG ADULT FACT BOOK

by

Janet M. Simons, Belva Finlay, and Alice Yang

> DEAR LORD
> BE GOOD TO ME
> THE SEA IS SO
> WIDE AND SO
> MY BOAT IS
> SO SMALL

Children's Defense Fund

Copyright©1991 by Children's Defense Fund.
All rights reserved.

ISBN: 0-938008-83-8
Library of Congress Catalog Card No.: 90-085743

Acknowledgments

The Adolescent and Young Adult Fact Book was written and produced with support from the Skillman Foundation of Detroit, Michigan. The Charles Revson Foundation provides support for all CDF publications.

The following persons, listed alphabetically, have contributed to the production of this book:

MaryLee Allen, Patricia Carroll, Brent Chism, Luis Duany, Celeste Garcia, Olivia Golden, Kati Haycock, David Heffernan, Donna M. Jablonski, Clifford Johnson, Kay Johnson, Janis Johnston, Karen Panton, Karen Pittman, Delia Pompa, Lisa Reckler, Sara Rosenbaum, Paul Smith, Stephen E. Wilhite, and Nancy Williams.

Contents

Executive Summary:
The Risks Facing Teenagers and Young Adults vii

Introduction and Recommendations:
Fateful Choices 1

What Works for Teens and Young Adults 17

Adolescents and Young Adults and Their Families 43

Health 57

Substance Abuse, Crime, and Victimization 73

Education 93

Employment, Earnings, and Income 115

Sexual Activity, Pregnancy, and Family Formation 127

Listing of Tables and Figures 145

EXECUTIVE SUMMARY
THE RISKS FACING TEENAGERS AND YOUNG ADULTS

Being a teenager today is far riskier than it ever has been. Many teens are poor and unhealthy, unsafe in their homes, their neighborhoods, and their schools. Many are at risk of drug or alcohol dependency, or become pregnant long before they are ready to become parents. And many are written off as unsalvageable by their schools. The consequences of youths' actions now include dangers ranging from single parenthood and prolonged poverty to AIDS to lifestyles of devastating violence.

Even those who live in comfortable middle-class circumstances are not shielded from risk. They spend less time with parents and other caring adults than did teenagers of earlier generations. They are bombarded by a barrage of cultural messages extolling materialism and casual sex. Many are attending schools that are only mediocre, and by the time they become high school seniors, many say they use alcohol every week. The consequences of these trends are increasingly grave.

What follows is a statistical profile of some the harshest realities of teenagers' lives. These statistics do not represent the experience of most adolescents, of course. In spite of the increased risks, most of America's teenagers manage to progress steadily and successfully through the traditional steps to adulthood: school completion, employment, marriage, and parenthood. Yet as a nation we lag behind many less developed countries in how we care for our young people. We cannot afford to turn our back on America's youths who stumble on the path to adulthood.

1. Unmarried teenagers are getting pregnant and having babies in alarming numbers.
- Birth rates among *unmarried* teenagers and young women are higher than they have ever been, even though birth rates for all teenaged girls have remained roughly stable since 1976.
- One million teenagers—about the equivalent of the entire population of San Antonio, Texas—got pregnant in 1988. The number of babies born to teenage mothers that same year—half a million—is equivalent to the entire population of Denver.
- Almost two-thirds of all births to teens are to unmarried girls, compared with less than one-third in 1970.
- More than 90 percent of births to black teens are to unmarried girls, but the relative increase in births to unmarried teens has been much greater among white girls than among blacks in the past two decades.
- Teenagers with the poorest basic academic skills are the most likely to have babies as teenagers.

2. Teenagers and young adults are dying violent deaths.
- A total of 5,771 young people between the ages of 15 and 24 were homicide victims in 1988. Put another way, there were 15 times more young casualties from violence here at home than there were total casualties from the Desert Shield and Desert Storm operations in the Persian Gulf.
- Homicide is the second leading cause of death among adolescents and young people ages 15 to 24. Motor vehicle accidents are the leading cause, and suicides are third.
- Black teenage males are three times more likely to be killed by guns than to die of natural causes.
- The firearm homicide rate for black males ages 15 to 19 more than doubled between 1984 and 1988, after see-sawing in a generally downward direction between 1979 and 1984. The period of sharp increase generally corresponds to the period when the crack trade and its accompanying violence began to dominate many urban black neighborhoods. In addition to the youths killed and injured in this violence, many more who have witnessed killings and known the victims are harmed indirectly.

3. **Alcohol use among teens begins early and is widespread.**
   - More than half of seventh- to twelfth-graders nationwide drink alcohol. Eight million—about 40 percent—drink weekly. Four million drink when they feel upset; more than 2 million drink because they are bored.
   - Daily drinking and binge drinking are common among high school seniors. More than 30 percent of high school seniors say they are binge drinkers, defined as having five drinks or more in a row.
   - In 1989, 2,800 teenagers ages 15 to 19 died in traffic crashes related to alcohol—more than all deaths reported in Alaska that year and four times the number of AIDS deaths among people younger than 25.
   - Teenage drinkers start drinking, on average, about age 13.

4. **Teens and young adults are still using illegal drugs.**
   - In 1990 almost one-quarter of surveyed 12- to 17-year-olds and more than half of 18- to 25-year-olds reported having used illicit drugs (drugs other than alcohol and tobacco) at some time in their lives. Although these figures represent a substantial drop in self-reported use since 1985, they are still very high, and they do not include information from runaway, incarcerated, or homeless youths, who are at great risk of drug abuse. The drop in casual use masks the persistence of drug addiction among older teens and young adults.
   - One in 15 teenagers and one in six young adults say they currently use both alcohol and illegal drugs.
   - High school seniors who don't plan to graduate from a four-year college are more likely to have used illegal drugs than their classmates who do.

5. **The drug trade and drug use are destroying teenagers' neighborhoods and drawing teenagers into crime and violence as never before.**
   - The arrest rate for drug offenses by 18-year-old males increased 15-fold between 1965 and 1975 and has fallen very little since then.
   - Since 1965 there has been a steady increase in the arrest rates of 18-year-old males for weapons violations.
   - The arrest rates of 18-year-olds for violent crime and property crime have doubled since 1965.
   - More than half of all committed juvenile offenders used alcohol or illegal drugs regularly before being imprisoned.
   - Forty percent of committed juvenile offenders were under

the influence of illegal drugs when they committed their most recent crime, and one-third were under the influence of alcohol.

6. Millions of teenagers are victims of crime.
- Teenage girls are the most likely victims of sexual abuse.
- Almost 1.8 million teens were victims of violent crimes in 1988, and 3.2 million were victims of theft.

7. Many teenagers' potential is stunted by the effects of inadequate family and community resources.
- A total of 3.2 million 12- to 17-year-olds live in poverty—equivalent to the entire population of Albania or Costa Rica and nearly equal the population of the city of Los Angeles.
- Poor adolescents and young adults are 50 percent more likely than nonpoor teens to have a physical or mental disability.
- Poor young adults—whatever their race or ethnic background—are three times more likely than their nonpoor peers to have dropped out of high school.
- Low-income teenagers are more likely to be victims of violence than other teens.
- Low-income youths are less than one-tenth as likely as their more affluent peers to earn a bachelor's degree within four years of high school graduation.

8. Black and Latino teenagers are shortchanged in school.
- One-third of all black and Latino students attend schools in which at least 90 percent of the students are from minority groups. Nationwide hearings in 1986-1987 documented that minority schools had high teacher turnover, few computers or up-to-date texts, and few special programs for gifted and talented students.
- Black and Latino teens are more likely than whites to be two or more grades behind in school.
- Black and Latino students are less likely than white and Asian students to attend schools with strong college preparatory programs and are less likely to be enrolled in academic programs.
- Black students are at least twice as likely as other students to be assigned to programs for the educable mentally retarded.
- Latino young adults are more than three times as likely to have dropped out of high school as white youths. Blacks

graduate at nearly the same rate as whites, but take longer to complete high school.

9. Many young workers are having difficulty earning enough to support a family.
- The median weekly wage of 18- to 24-year-old men plummeted 20 percent between 1979 and 1989, after accounting for inflation.
- Young women still earn less than young men. A female with some college education earns only slightly more than a male high school graduate with no college education.
- Black young adults are about twice as likely as their white counterparts to be unable to find full-time work.
- As income has dropped, so have marriage rates, a trend that some sociologists say is predictable when young men's earnings decline. Between 1970 and 1989, the proportion of young adults ages 20 to 24 who had ever been married dropped by 23 percentage points for men and 28 points for women.

These findings are troubling in themselves. They are truly alarming in light of the demographic changes in our population that are making adolescents and young adults an increasingly scarce resource. Our nation cannot afford to sacrifice the contributions of any our young people to the effects of poverty, violence, drug and alcohol abuse, premature pregnancy and childrearing, and inadequate education.
- The young work force is expected to shrink 14 percent in the decade between 1985 and 1995. There will be almost 4.5 million fewer 18- to 24-year-olds in 1995 than in 1985.
- The proportion of teens and young adults in the black, Latino, Native American, Eskimo, and other minority populations is higher than in the white population, meaning that our future young work force will have a larger proportion of minority workers than in the past. In general, minority teens are the most likely to be disadvantaged in ways that hinder future productivity in the work place.
- Black and Latino adolescents are concentrated in the central cities, which have fewer social services, poorer schools, and more substandard housing than the suburbs, where white teens are likely to live.

All of these realities mean that far too many adolescents enter adulthood poorly equipped to meet their responsibilities as parents, citizens, and members of the work force. For their sake, and for the sake of the nation's future, America must act.

INTRODUCTION AND RECOMMENDATIONS

FATEFUL CHOICES

Today's teenagers are a lot like yesterday's teenagers, but the world around them has changed drastically.

Thirty years ago, a teenager who dropped out of school often could find a job that paid a living wage and look forward to earning enough in the future to support a family. Today, a high school dropout has only one chance in three of having a full-time job. A typical male high school dropout between the ages of 18 and 24 earns only about $6,000 a year, and a young female dropout earns even less.

Forty years ago, a young woman who had a child at 17 was likely to be married, and her husband was likely to have a job. Today she is most likely to be single and to be unprepared to support her family. More than 80 percent of single black mothers younger than 25 and more than 70 percent of single white mothers in the same age group are poor.

The world of twenty-first century America will demand far more education, creativity, and adaptability from young citizens than ever before. To become productive workers, capable parents, and informed citizens, adolescents must use the teen years to equip themselves for the challenges ahead.

Yet today's teenagers, like adolescents of every generation, tend to live only for the moment. They take risks, test limits, and make shortsighted judgments. These behaviors are a necessary part of maturing, but the consequences can be much more serious than they used to be.

THE ADOLESCENT AND YOUNG ADULT FACT BOOK

One Day in the Lives of American Youths

Every day seven teenagers and 10 young adults are the victims of homicide.

Every day 10 teenagers and 13 young adults are killed by firearms.

Every day 39 youths ages 15 to 24 are killed in motor vehicle accidents.

Every day 604 teenagers contract syphilis or gonorrhea.

Every day an estimated 1,140 teenagers have abortions.

Every day teenagers give birth to 1,336 babies and teens younger than 15 give birth to 29 babies.

Every day of the school year 2,478 teenagers drop out of school.

Every day 4,901 teenagers and 2,976 young adults are the victims of violent crime.

Every day 7,742 teenagers become sexually active.

Every day 8,826 teenagers and 6,235 young adults are the victims of theft.

◆ ◆ ◆ ◆ ◆

134,000 teenagers use cocaine once a week or more.

580,000 teenagers use marijuana once a week or more.

454,000 junior and senior high school students are weekly binge drinkers.

8 million junior and senior high school students drink alcohol weekly.

Every month an average of 1.1 million teenagers and 1.2 million young adults are unemployed.

CHILDREN'S DEFENSE FUND

Until the last decade, unprotected sex might lead to pregnancy, but it was not likely to lead to death. By March 1991, however, more than 34,000 20- through 29-year-olds had been diagnosed with AIDS. The lag time between HIV infection and the onset of AIDS suggests that many of these young adults were infected with the fatal disease as teens.

Thirty years ago, feuding teenage boys might get into a fist fight. Today, in some neighborhoods, they shoot each other. Teenage boys now are more likely to die from gunshot wounds than from all natural causes combined. The number of male homicide victims ages 15 to 24 in 1988 was more than twice the total number of major league baseball, basketball, football, and hockey players in the United States.

By the time they reach adolescence many children already have experienced a level of violence that only combat soldiers used to know. When a group of 500 children in Southside Chicago was asked about violence in their neighborhood, 26 percent said they had seen someone shot, and 29 percent had seen a stabbing.

While their environment has become more threatening, teenagers have become less connected to their families. Just 63 percent of families with children eat dinner together frequently. Almost one in five surveyed sixth- through twelfth-graders reported that they had not had a 10-minute conversation with one of their parents within the previous month. In 1988, 127,000 children—most of them teenagers—were thrown out of their homes by their parents or were refused permission to return home after they ran away.

Adolescence also lasts longer and is more ambiguous these days, partly because children are maturing physically at earlier ages, and partly because it takes more schooling and job experience to become economically independent. Many young employed adults—including college graduates in their mid-twenties—are living with their parents because their paychecks can't cover today's high rents, living expenses, and student loan payments all at the same time.

As challenging as it is for teenagers as a whole, the path to adulthood is even more difficult for poor and minority teenagers. Black youths, for example, are two to three times as likely as white youths to be victims of handgun crimes. One-third of Latino teenagers lack medical insurance and probably are not getting basic health or dental care. And the education of minority students is generally so inadequate that the average 17-year-old black or Latino student can read and do math no better than the average white 13-year-old.

Despite the hazards, the vast majority of America's teenagers do arrive at adulthood full of hope and promise. Parents, schools, and neighborhoods are managing—often with scarce resources—to make sure most teens have the guidance and opportunities they need to prepare for the future. Yet America must do better. *All* adolescents must get the help that will lead them to productive, satisfying adult lives.

As the proportion of young people in our population drops, we need every young adult to perform at top capacity. In 1950 there were 17 people at work to support each retired person; by 1992 there will be only three workers for every retiree. By 2030, the number of senior citizens will equal the number of teens and young adults. If we allow even a small proportion of these young people to reach adulthood unhealthy, unskilled, or alienated, the nation will be dangerously short on the energy and creativity necessary to maintain America's standard of living and leadership role in the world.

Key facts about black teens

A black male teenager between the ages of 15 and 19 is nine times more likely than his white peer to be a homicide victim.

A black female teenager is more than twice as likely as her white peer to have a baby.

A black teenager is more than twice as likely as a white teenager to be enrolled in a remedial math class.

A black high school graduate is only half as likely as a white graduate to receive a bachelor's degree four years after high school.

One black teenager in every two lives with only one parent.

One black teenager in every three lives with a parent who did not graduate from high school.

One black teenager in every three lives with an unemployed parent.

About 400,000 young people dropped out of high school between October 1989 and October 1990. One in three of them is unemployed. Each year's high school dropouts ultimately cost the nation about $340 billion in lost productivity and lost tax revenue. That amount of money is 50 percent more than the nation's total yearly expenditure on education, including public and private education at all levels—preschool, elementary, secondary, and postsecondary. And that doesn't even include the expense of the long-term welfare assistance that some of these dropouts will need, or the $20,000 or more a year it will cost to imprison each dropout who gets into serious trouble with the law.

Yet there is no mystery about how to avoid such a waste of our young people's potential. We know, first of all, that every teenager needs the basics: nurturing families, basic health care, adequate food and shelter, and good schools. Right now more than 18 percent of our six- to 17-year-olds live in poverty, which means many adolescents lack the necessary building blocks of healthy development. Americans are beginning to understand the importance of giving very young children these basics, but we often forget that adolescents must have them too. When teenagers' families don't have adequate

Key facts about Latino teens

A Latino teenager is twice as likely as a white teenager to have no health insurance.

Sixteen- and 17-year-old Latina girls are four times more likely than their white peers to be behind in school.

Male Latino 18- and 19-year-olds are five times more likely than their white peers to be behind in school.

Latino 18- and 19-year-olds are more than twice as likely as their white peers to be school dropouts.

One Latino teenager in every two lives with a parent who did not graduate from high school.

One Latino teenager in every four lives with an unemployed parent.

resources to meet their children's basic needs, it is vital to the nation's future that our public systems supplement the families' efforts.

Second, teenagers need help understanding and integrating the tremendous physical, emotional, social, and other developmental changes they experience during adolescence. Every institution that deals with teenagers—families, religious institutions, schools, health care systems, child welfare and juvenile justice systems, and youth organizations—must improve their ability to respond to the particular developmental needs of adolescents.

Third, teenagers need regular opportunities to explore options and broaden their perceptions of what their lives can be. We must offer them opportunities to set specific goals for themselves and enjoy the satisfaction of accomplishing them. We must offer activities in which they can develop their leadership and decision-making skills. We must be sure they have safe environments in which to try out new behaviors and have fun.

Families traditionally have been the source of all of these supports, and many families continue to fulfill this role. As our society and our economy become more complex, however, more and more parents must depend on schools and other community resources to help them prepare their teenagers for the future. Therefore every community needs to develop a network of programs and services for young people that can support and supplement the nurturing and guidance teenagers receive at home.

The stress on teens is especially strong at times of transition—from elementary to middle school, from middle school to high school, and from high school to the next phase of life, whatever it may be. Yet our social and educational institutions generally don't provide enough extra supports at these stressful junctures. We need to focus more resources on transition periods, when youngsters are especially vulnerable to discouragement, negative self-image, peer pressure, and confusion about the future.

Finally, we must provide special help and encouragement for our most vulnerable teenagers. They include many teens who are poor or homeless, in foster care, or in the juvenile justice system, and many who come from minority groups or have physical, mental, or emotional disabilities. Adolescence is especially perilous for youths who live in violent neighborhoods and never feel completely safe, for youths who don't have the security of a stable family life, or for those who have been shunned by classmates for living in a shelter or coming from a different culture.

Because teens have such a variety of needs and there are so many opportunities for them to fall through the cracks, every sector of our society must play a part in launching teenagers into successful adulthood. Now, more than ever before, the old saying is true: it does take a village to raise a child. We can't count on a strong national future unless our families, communities, and all levels of government work together to help our teenagers make a successful transition to adulthood.

Many people in many communities already are working to help teens navigate around the perils of adolescence. Some

---

What Must Be Done to Save Our Teens

Six areas are extremely important in bolstering the motivation and capacity of teens to make wise choices about their futures and to prevent too-early pregnancy, substance abuse, crime, and violence:

■ **Education and strong basic skills.** Youths who are behind a grade or have poor basic skills or poor attendance are at high risk of early parenthood. Low-income and minority teens have higher rates of school failure.

■ **A range of non-academic opportunities for success.** Children and teens need to feel good about themselves. They need a clear vision of a successful and self-sufficient future. Self-sufficiency potential is related to self-esteem and self-perception. For youths who are not doing well in school, non-academic avenues for success are crucial.

■ **Links to caring adults who provide positive role models, values, and support for teens.** Parents are the most important sources of guidance and nurturing for children of all ages, and our society needs to support parents in this role. In addition, a relationship with a caring adult outside the family can have an extraordinary impact on a

continued on next page

of their inspiring efforts, which offer ideas for all communities to draw on, are described in this book's What Works for Teens and Young Adults chapter.

Yet individual programs, however extraordinary, can't bear the entire burden of making sure all teenagers get their needs met. As a nation we must invest more attention and resources in supporting the full development of our young people. The following discussion highlights key actions for national and state governments as well as broad community-wide approaches that go far beyond single programs.

---

continued from page 7

teenager, whether that adult is a teacher, a school counselor, a professional youth worker, a religious congregation member, a volunteer in a mentoring program, or simply a neighbor.

■ **Family life education and life planning.** All teens need sexuality and parenting education as well as help in understanding the impact of present choices in planning their futures. Parents, schools, and religious institutions need to communicate more effectively with the young about sexuality.

■ **Comprehensive adolescent health services.** A range of comprehensive and convenient services are needed for teens in a range of settings.

■ **A basic standard of living for all teens and their families, including access to jobs, nutrition, housing, income, and services to meet special needs.** Teens growing up in poverty more often become teen parents and experience a variety of other ills in adolescence and early adulthood than those growing up in families with more support for basic needs. And as teens grow up and start their own families, access to jobs, work-related skill training, food, and shelter for these young families is crucial to the healthy development of the next generation of youngsters.

Saving our teenagers: A blueprint for action

In order to make sure every American teenager makes a successful transition to adulthood, our nation must build on our knowledge of what works for teens. We know a great deal about what works to bolster the motivation and capacity of teens to prevent too-early pregnancy, and the experience of committed professionals who work with teens suggests that the same principles help to prevent other risky and self-defeating behaviors such as substance abuse, crime, and violence.

1. Education and strong basic skills

The first key principle for enabling teens to make a successful transition to adulthood, avoiding too-early pregnancy, and other risky choices, is to **give every teenager a first-rate education and the chance to experience academic success.**

- *Rigorous education.* Every teenager must be academically prepared for the future. Regardless of race, ethnic origin, income, or gender, every American student must study a rigorous curriculum taught by skilled and committed teachers. Students with disabilities and non-English-speaking students should receive the special help they need to achieve academically.

- *Ambitious education and career goals.* As the world of work becomes more complex, schools must develop far better education and career counseling programs that promote college or high-quality post-high school training as a real option for every student. Schools must monitor their students' progress to be sure each one receives the academic preparation necessary to achieve ambitious education and career goals.

- *Student loans, grants, and scholarships.* If every teenager and young adult is to have access to the education needed today to become a fully contributing and self-sufficient adult, we must provide a system of loans and grants that ensures that no young person is forced to cut short his or her education for financial reasons.

- *Effective counseling and links to community services.* We recommend that schools become referral and delivery sites for coordinated social services for teenagers and their families. We also recommend that schools increase the numbers of trained guidance counselors who are available to students. These counselors should be advocates for students, committed to working closely with students' families and to involving parents in their teenagers' education.

2. A range of non-academic opportunities for success

To ensure that teenagers have opportunities to build the self-confidence and self-esteem that lead to good choices about the future, we must **give every teenager opportunities to participate in recreation programs, organized social and cultural activities, and community service programs.**

- *Recreational and social activities.* Every teenager should participate in extracurricular activities that bring him or her into contact with caring adults and supportive peers and provide constructive recreational and social outlets for adolescent energy. These activities should be offered through thoughtfully structured youth programs designed to meet youths' developmental needs. Communities that provide little more than unsupervised sports fields for teenagers are missing valuable opportunities to fill youths' leisure time with growth-enhancing experiences. Each community must find ways to increase the resources available for quality youth programs, especially in low-income neighborhoods, where they are most likely to be scarce. (See the What Works for Teens and Young Adults chapter for examples of various types of effective youth programs.)

- *Religious and cultural enrichment.* Appropriate groups in every community should develop youth programs designed to promote teenagers' understanding of and pride in their cultural or religious roots. Teenagers gain self-confidence and a stronger sense of themselves when they have opportunities to celebrate their cultural identity.

- *Community service opportunities.* Every teenager should have an opportunity to participate in carefully designed community service activities. Contributing constructively to the community and helping others give teenagers a stake in the common good and boost confidence and self-esteem. Community service programs should give teens meaningful tasks and frequent interactions with other teens as well as adults, and include regular opportunities to reflect on and discuss their activities.

3. Links to caring adults who provide positive role models, values, and support for teens

To combat the fragmentation, isolation, and stress of life for too many of today's teenagers, we must **make sure that all teens have regular contact with adults who believe in them and can help them broaden their options and plan for the future.**

■ ***Support for teens' families.*** Parents are the most important source of guidance and nurturing for children of all ages. But raising children can be difficult and frustrating, and many parents need help in meeting the challenge. The more our society can do to fortify families, the more likely our teenagers will grow up to fulfill their potential.

We recommend that all parents have access to family resource centers, parent support groups, and various parent education activities where they can discuss the challenges of raising children and get help with their special concerns. Family support programs are developing in many communities. However, like Missouri's Parents as Teachers program, which is available to every parent in the state, most of these programs are designed primarily to help parents of young children. Schools, business and religious organizations, and neighborhood youth centers should sponsor parent support and education activities that address the particular challenges facing parents of teens.

■ ***Intensive family-based services for families in crisis.*** Every state should develop intensive home-based crisis intervention services and other services designed to prevent the unnecessary placement of youths in out-of-home care. Although some children must be removed from their homes for their own or the community's protection, many more could safely remain at home if their families were assisted in getting the help necessary to better support and nurture them. New York, Missouri, and Michigan are among the states that have targeted family preservation services for youths at imminent risk of placement in the child welfare or juvenile justice systems.

■ ***Regular contact with caring adults outside the family.*** Every teenager needs a personal relationship with a caring adult to counsel him or her about career opportunities and life options. If a youth's parents are not equipped to play this role, he or she should have access to a teacher, a school counselor, a professional youth worker, a church member, or a volunteer in a mentoring program who can offer guidance. School counselors should make sure that every student has at least one adult mentor.

4. Family life education and life planning

To give teenagers the knowledge and the skills they need to make their own choices wisely in an increasingly risky world, parents, schools, health care providers, and religious and youth organizations all must **take responsibility for educat-**

ing young teenagers to reject self-destructive and dangerous behaviors. Many of today's teenagers first experiment with tobacco, alcohol, illicit drugs, and sex when they are very young. Teenage smokers start, on average, before the age of 12, and teenage drinkers start drinking at about 13. Young people who smoke and drink often experiment with illegal drugs and premature and unprotected sex as well.

■ *Education to reduce risk-taking.* Adolescents need information and instruction both in and outside of school about the serious consequences of alcohol and drug use, and too-early and unprotected sex. They also need to participate in activities that enhance self-esteem and self-control and help them resist peer pressure and media messages that glamorize risky behavior. Systematic instruction and discussion coupled with role playing have been effective in developing teens' ability to express disapproval and assert their own values. (See the What Works for Teens and Young Adults chapter for examples of how youth programs fill these needs.)

5. Comprehensive adolescent health services

To ensure that teenagers grow into healthy adults, we must **make sure that every teen has access to high quality, comprehensive health care that is responsive to the special needs of adolescents.**

■ *Adolescent health clinics.* We recommend that all middle and high schools develop adolescent health care programs, either alone or in cooperation with local health agencies, community health centers, or community hospitals. These programs should be located on or near school campuses and housing projects. It is especially critical for schools serving low-income students to establish clinics, because these students are unlikely to have a regular source of routine health care. All Medicaid programs should be required to cover the services of school-affiliated health programs.

■ *Universal health insurance coverage.* The nation should enact health care reform that provides health insurance coverage for every child and adolescent. Every child must receive basic preventive services such as routine health exams and dental care as well as treatment for physical, mental, and developmental health problems. At a minimum, the Medicaid program should be expanded immediately to cover all children and young adults to age 21 with family incomes below 200 percent of the federal poverty level.

6. A basic standard of living for all teens and their families, including access to jobs, nutrition, housing, income, and services to meet special needs

Both young people living with their parents and those in their late teens or early twenties who have formed their own families need access to jobs and a decent standard of living. We must **ensure that every youth has the opportunity to find a promising career path and become a self-sufficient adult, and that every young family has the economic support to ensure decent food and shelter for parents and children.** We must not exclude from these opportunities teens who have special needs, grow up in troubled families, or spend time in foster care or other out-of-home settings.

■ *Help in making the transition from school to work.* Schools and local businesses must collaborate to motivate students to complete high school and to increase employment rates among recent graduates. Students who do not plan to continue their education after high school are most likely to study and graduate from high school if they have help identifying entry-level jobs and training opportunities for competent high school graduates. These students also need access to school-to-work transition programs that include counseling, peer support, and job training and job placement assistance.

■ *Job skills, "second chance" education, and vocational training.* Every state and school district must develop second chance programs for high school dropouts and young adults who graduate with poor basic academic skills. These programs should combine individualized counseling and support services with remedial education and vocational training. The most successful federal program of this nature is the Job Corps, which returns $1.45 in benefits to society for every $1 invested in the program. We recommend that the Job Corps be expanded to serve far greater numbers of disadvantaged young people.

In addition, high school graduates not going on to college should have access to a wide range of vocational training options that prepare them for careers in better-paying, high-skill occupations. Federal and state governments as well as local communities should develop new approaches that combine this training with traditional educational activities, including youth apprenticeship programs, collaborative relationships between high schools and community colleges, and other longer term training options that lead to recognized credentials in sizable or growing occupational areas.

■ ***Continuum of services for special needs.*** The federal and state governments must provide sufficient funding to allow communities to establish a continuum of home- and community-based treatment programs for teenagers with special needs and their families. Treatment should be available for abused adolescents and others with emotional problems, for teenagers with other disabilities, and for those with drug and alcohol problems. These programs should involve the whole family when appropriate, and should address the social, emotional, educational, and physical health of the participants. Runaway and homeless youths and those in the custody of the child welfare and juvenile justice systems must not be neglected.

■ ***Transitional assistance for teens in out-of-home care.*** Teenagers who have grown up in a succession of foster homes or group care settings or have spent time in juvenile justice institutions need extra help when they are discharged from care. Frequently these youths have no families to return to. They need specific help learning the skills that are necessary to live independently as well as general support and encouragement to help them overcome the traumas of the past and develop the self-confidence to succeed.

■ ***Support for teen parents.*** Teenagers who become parents before they finish school face a difficult future. But with enough help and encouragement, these young mothers and fathers can become nurturing parents, continue their education, and prepare for self-sufficiency. Teen mothers and fathers should have access to support programs that offer long-term job and career counseling, parent education, and child care while they continue their schooling. One important goal of such programs must be to encourage teen parents to delay a second pregnancy until they have finished their education or training and are capable of supporting their family.

■ ***Child tax credit and child support insurance.*** The consequences for teens of growing up poor can be devastating: young people who grow up in poverty are more likely to do badly in school, have a range of health problems, and bear children early than those from more comfortably off families. Further, as teens and young adults form their own families, the impact of poverty on their young children can be devastating in turn. While jobs and job skills are a key part of the answer, recent economic changes have made it difficult for young workers to support a family even when they are working full time. In 1989, for example, nearly half of all hourly workers younger than 25 were paid wages too low to lift a family of three out of poverty.

Therefore, along with job skills and job opportunities, other key steps to eliminate poverty among children and teenagers include enactment of a child tax credit and child support insurance. A refundable tax credit to families with children and teenagers would provide a modest amount of assistance through the tax system to every family in recognition of the costs and responsibilities they bear in raising children and preparing them for adulthood. The economic foundation for families provided by this tax credit should be supplemented by a system of child support insurance that would insure children and teenagers against a parent's desertion or divorce, much in the same way that the federal government now insures many Americans against death and disability. When absent parents are not able to make adequate payments, or when federal or state governments fail to collect such support, the federal government would make up the difference to guarantee that children do not lose basic income support.

WHAT WORKS FOR TEENS AND YOUNG ADULTS

What makes some programs and services successful for young people while others make little difference? In Within Our Reach: Breaking the Cycle of Disadvantage, *author Lisbeth B. Schorr identifies "attributes of interventions that work" for disadvantaged children and families, including the following:*

- They provide a range of services, recognizing that a single intervention cannot combat a comprehensive range of problems. A youth's survival needs, for food or shelter, for example, may have to be addressed before he or she can benefit from a dropout prevention service.
- They are flexible, with services based on the judgment of professionals who understand the needs of individual program participants.
- Staff members care about, respect, and are trusted by those who receive services.
- Services are coherent, easy-to-use, have continuity, are offered at times and places appropriate for youths, and are not crippled by bureaucratic obstacles.

When it comes to interventions that target teens in particular, program operators and evaluators repeatedly cite one additional "must": programs must treat teens as adults, recognize that teens want to feel needed, and turn that desire into constructive action.

Further, CDF has identified six areas of intervention that are critical for youths:

- Education and strong basic skills.
- Jobs, work-related skills building, and work exposure.
- A range of non-academic opportunities for success.

- Family life education and life planning.
- Comprehensive adolescent health services.
- A national and community climate that makes teen development and teen pregnancy prevention a leading priority.

The following programs, presented as examples rather than as an attempt to list effective programs comprehensively, illustrate some of these attributes. Because most of these programs are relatively new and their results often are hard to measure, they have not all been evaluated formally. Nonetheless they offer a wealth of ideas and experiences on which communities can draw.

The Valued Youth Program: Turning "problem" students into resources

Educators in several Texas school districts have stopped just telling their problem students to do better. They've given them a real reason to.

The educators are taking middle school students who seem headed for dropout and giving them the task of tutoring elementary school students. The idea is that if young people are to succeed in school, they must feel good about themselves and about school, and the best way for adults to nurture these positive attitudes in students is to make them feel valued. The Texas educators also are convinced that like anyone, students learn their subjects better if they have to teach them to others.

Four days a week, during one period of the day, students in the Valued Youth Program (VYP) in San Antonio and McAllen, Texas, walk or ride a bus with a teacher to a nearby elementary school. Each tutor works in a classroom with three children on math and reading and stays with the same group all year. At the end of the period the tutors return to the middle school and continue with the rest of their day. On the fifth day, the tutors gather with the VYP teacher at their own school to discuss tutoring skills, reflect on the week's work, or brush up on their own literacy skills. Several times a year the tutors go on field trips that expose them to cultural and future career opportunities in the broader community.

For their work the tutors get course credit and minimum wage pay, plus a greater sense of self-worth, better grades, and a more positive outlook on school and teachers. The younger children also benefit, getting extra help with school work and interacting regularly with important role models.

To be sure, the idea of entrusting so-called "at-risk" students with tutoring responsibilities makes some people nervous. But that's before they see the results.

Ana was a 14-year-old eighth-grader who "never even wanted to come to school. I used to think it was boring and it wasn't important for me." Ana's parents, born in Mexico, both have less than an eighth-grade education. Ana seemed destined for school failure. But after a year in VYP, Ana's grades in math, reading, and English jumped from Ds to As. Her parents say she is more responsible now, helping her brothers and sisters with school work and contributing her entire tutoring paycheck toward paying the family's bills. Ana wants to finish high school and go to college.

Ana's not an exception. Since VYP began in 1984, nearly 800 tutors and 2,000 elementary school students in eight school districts have participated. Evaluations have shown that, overall, these students have improved their grades, gained greater self-pride, and developed better attitudes toward school than similar students not in the program.

VYP seems especially effective in keeping students in school. Between 1988 and 1990, one tutor out of 101 (or 1 percent) dropped out of school, compared with 11 out of 93 (or 12 percent) in a comparison group of similar students who did not participate in the program.

"Tutoring helps me come to school because I have to come and teach the kids," says one VYP participant. "I don't miss too many days because the students ask me where I've been, and tell me that they miss me. Every time I'm absent...they ask me, 'Where were you?' I really like those kids. If I hadn't been a tutor, I would have missed more school."

What makes a program like VYP work, says program director Maria del Refugio Robledo, is the fact that students are treated as talented resources rather than as problems. At VYP, the positive message is reinforced by year-end recognition events where tutors are given certificates, T-shirts, or other tokens of appreciation. Recently several tutors served as hosts and hostesses for a PTA meeting — jobs traditionally reserved for honor students.

It's also important that participants are paid — not to be in school, but for their tutoring work, Robledo is quick to point out. These days schools have to be willing to provide or broker services to meet students' needs, whether or not the services are deemed part of "education," she says. In the case of VYP students and their families, these needs often are economic. According to Robledo, programs similar to VYP that do not pay their tutors have been less successful.

As for challenges, one of the biggest is creating a school climate in which parents feel welcome. It's well known that students generally do better in school if their parents are involved in school activities. But because of culture and language differences, many minority students' family and school lives never mix. VYP has found that parents are much more likely to get involved if students plan and set up their own school events—a potluck dinner, for example—and "pester" their parents to come. Teachers and administrators can do a lot to increase parents' interest, too, by calling them with good news about their children's work in the program.

VYP was funded originally by Coca-Cola USA and later by the U.S. Department of Education. In April 1991, the latter's Program Effectiveness Panel approved VYP, meaning there is convincing evidence of the program's effectiveness. Not surprisingly, interest in the VYP model is spreading beyond Texas borders. With a new grant from the Coca-Cola Foundation, the program will expand in the 1991-1992 school year to California, New York, and Florida.

For more information, contact Maria del Refugio Robledo, Intercultural Development Research Association, 5835 Callaghan, Suite 350, San Antonio, TX 78228, (512) 684-8180.

The Youth Action Program: Building their futures

For years the gutted building at Second Avenue and 119th Street in East Harlem stood dark and useless. Then a group of teenagers took tools to it, determined to turn it into decent apartments for homeless young families.

Four years later, after the work of nearly 200 local youths, the building housed four modest but modern and clean apartments with double paned windows and sanded wood floors and was ready to receive tenants.

That first building was completed in 1983. Since then the hundreds of young people, mostly school dropouts, who have rolled through East Harlem's Youth Action Program have renovated three other abandoned buildings into apartments and community centers for the poor. They've also attended basic skills and GED preparation classes in the program and taken part in workshops, counseling, and special activities to pick up "life skills"—anything from driving a car to getting to work on time to making responsible sexuality decisions. Many of the youths, armed with construction and carpentry skills they learned while working on the buildings, have moved on to apprenticeships or full-time jobs in the building trade. Others have gone back to school or vocational training.

It's the Youth Action Program's way of dealing with youth unemployment, homelessness, and neighborhood deterioration. Sixteen- to 24-year-olds who need jobs, job skills, and a second chance at education join up for six to 18 months. They spend half their time in closely supervised, paid work rehabilitating buildings and the other half in classrooms working on academic skills. The point is to improve their community while improving their own chances for a decent future. At the end of their stay, the program tries to place them in full-time jobs, which turn out usually to be fairly well-paying construction work.

From time to time while they're in the program, these young people also meet with state and local legislators, attend budget hearings, speak out at public meetings, or go on vigils to advocate support for youth employment and community improvement initiatives. Often the youths themselves identify issues in the community that need to be addressed—for example, employment funding, drugs, or gang violence—and come up with advocacy angles.

The idea of combining physical neighborhood improvement, youth employment, and advocacy by youths for youths is so logical and appealing that communities across the nation have joined forces and created a national coalition to replicate the Youth Action Program model. Called the YouthBuild Coalition and headquartered in Belmont, Massachusetts, the group officially began in 1988 and since has signed on 200 organizations in 35 states that support replication and advocacy work in various ways. Of the 200, 18 actually have launched their own programs following the YouthBuild design, and another 60 or so are in planning and fund raising stages. One of the coalition's biggest pushes now as a group is for Congress to pass the YouthBuild Act, which would authorize $200 million for YouthBuild programs administered through the U.S. Department of Housing and Urban Development.

YouthBuild's growing popularity reflects not just the grownups' belief that it's a good idea, but the enthusiasm of the young people, too. The coalition's founder Dorothy Stoneman says that every time a YouthBuild program puts an ad in the paper, it draws seven times more applicants than it can accept. "Young people feel deep satisfaction about building housing for the homeless because it allows them to make a real contribution to the community," says Stoneman, who also co-founded the Youth Action Program.

And although not everyone who comes into the program knows he or she wants a construction career, says Stoneman, everyone wants to do good for the community and do well for themselves. It then becomes the program's job to provide the skills, support, and good relationships each young person needs to sustain that enthusiasm.

Judging from some recent YouthBuild "graduates," these programs do that pretty well. James joined the program in New York in 1987 as a high school dropout. Although he was bright, he had little confidence and was very quiet, recalls Stoneman. Eighteen months later, he had a GED, a driver's license, and solid carpentry skills. With help from the Youth Action Program, he set up a carpentry company with 15 other graduates. The company lasted only two years, but by then James had enough know-how to go it alone. He started another company, now still running. "Without [the YouthBuild project] you don't know what he would've found," says Stoneman.

Making a YouthBuild program work takes all the basics like a committed staff, good management, and strong leadership. In addition, though, YouthBuild makes a strong point of involving participants in decision making at every level—from policy directions to what kind of bricks to use. The Youth Action Program was co-founded, in fact, by the youths who became its first enrollees. Today half of the 14-member Steering Committee of the national YouthBuild Coalition are young people elected from the various local projects throughout the country.

There also has to be equal emphasis on all program aspects. At the building sites, for example, the goal isn't just to get the job done quickly—although that's important—but to make sure the trainees learn real skills. That means, for one thing, that the young people get to do all the construction tasks, not just the easy ones. And within the program as a whole, the point still isn't just to teach the trainees practical construction skills, but to help them make academic gains and develop leadership potential as well, and to teach them life skills and nurture their self-esteem.

It's a tall order indeed, made taller by the constant challenges of finding funding, piecing together money from local private and public groups and federal job training, community development, and vocational education programs. Still, the YouthBuild concept seems to be catching on, and when it comes to finding financial support, say the coalition's advocates, you just don't take no for an answer.

For more information, contact the YouthBuild Coalition, 366 Marsh St., Belmont, MA 02178, (617) 489-3400.

City Lights: A special school for troubled youths

"Troubled" may be understating it. Terry, a 17-year-old, was referred to City Lights by his parole officer while he was in juvenile detention for his fourth criminal offense: fencing stolen goods. Previous charges included car theft and breaking and entering. Terry lives with his mother, four siblings, his sister's baby, and his mother's male companion, who sometimes gets violent when he is drunk. Terry has normal intelligence but reads at third-grade level. One minute he swaggers with seeming self-confidence, the next he sinks into deep sadness.

At City Lights school in Washington, D.C., young people like Terry—written off by schools, courts, and social workers as unteachable, intractable, and untreatable—are getting another chance. About 100 14- to 21-year-olds are enrolled in the school, which features remedial education, GED and college preparation, extensive clinical and psychological services, vocational counseling and job placement, and substance abuse prevention and treatment. The school works to enable its students to lead independent, productive lives by helping them develop both academic and work place competencies. Funding for the program comes from District government agencies, federal grants, and contributions from the United Way and various foundations.

In some ways City Lights is much like any regular school. Students come five days a week, they go to classes, some serve on the student council or play on the school's basketball team.

But everything else is different. The typical student is a disadvantaged foster child years behind in school and suffering deep emotional problems. Many have histories of physical or sexual abuse, neglect, delinquency, or drug abuse. Every aspect of City Lights is specially designed, therefore, to create "an environment that guarantees the novelty of success to experts at failure," as founder Judith Tolmach Silber puts it.

The educational component, for example, relies on a self-paced computer-assisted learning package that teaches academics as well as practical living skills. The instruction is adapted for a full range of reading levels, so that someone like Terry could learn about nutrition, say, through instructions written at a third-grade reading level. The computer also breaks the instruction into bite-sized chunks so students can gauge their progress continuously and gain frequent feelings of accomplishment. And rather than replacing teachers, the system allows teachers to give students more individualized help.

The constant therapeutic interactions at City Lights are unlike anything its students are likely to find in other schools, even most other alternative schools or mental health institutions. Individual therapy, group therapy, family counseling, and clinical meetings "packaged" into an individualized treatment plan are a part of every student's life. Because drug abuse is so prevalent among its students, the school has set up a special program of drug abuse counseling, health and physical education, and drug and alcohol monitoring. Over the years the staff also has experimented with various kinds of music, art, and sports therapy.

Students also get counseling whenever they need it. For example, one student's case manager met with her every morning before school. At these brief but timely meetings, the student expressed her anger and sadness, and the therapist helped her understand her feelings and coached her on behavior—all before she entered the classroom.

City Lights' results so far have been encouraging: Despite a population of chronic truants, the 600-plus students who have enrolled since 1982 have had an average attendance rate of more than 85 percent. On average they have gained more than one grade level for every six months of instruction. Eighty-six percent of all graduates stay out of hospitals, jails, and other institutions for up to two years.

Many say it's the staff that really makes City Lights work. Teaching or counseling at City Lights is a lot more than helping students work a lesson or decide what kind of career they might want. It's realizing that City Lights may be the last chance for these young people to avoid failure and then doing whatever they need, from acting as liaison between students and their families or social service agencies, to getting a student a new pair of eyeglasses. In the classroom, acting out and yelling at teachers are expected student behavior. But the staff stays on course, coaxing, nurturing, insisting. If there is any magic to City Lights' success, it is, according to Silber, "a trusting relationship that develops with painstaking slowness between students, teachers, and clinicians."

Eventually, some of the most resistant students come around. "I messed up when I first came to City Lights," says a former student. "I didn't want to go to school. Teachers would say stuff to me and I would argue with them. 'I don't need you,' I would say. But the teachers pushed me. They kept on telling me, 'You're going to be somebody.'...Finally I began to listen. I said, 'I gotta change.'"

It costs $10,000 a year to keep one young person at City Lights. To some that may seem like a lot. But it's far less than the $50,000 it costs to keep the same young person in jail, points out City Lights staff, and jail usually doesn't turn out people who believe in their ability to succeed.

For more information, contact City Lights School, 724 Ninth St., N.W., Suite 420, Washington, DC 20001, (202) 347-5010.

STEP: Summer Training and Education Program

Two years ago Dashelle Jackson, then 14, of the Belle Glade public housing project in Palm Beach, Florida, was making Cs and Ds in school. She was shy and afraid to raise her hand, speak up in class, or interact with others. She was at risk of dropping out. Her life turned around when she completed the Summer Training and Education Program (STEP).

Now operating in about 100 sites around the country, STEP is part of each community's school dropout prevention effort. It works with disadvantaged 14- and 15-year-olds, who come from a variety of racial and ethnic backgrounds. The program combines a half day of reading and math classes and life skills instruction with half-time work under the federal Summer Youth Employment and Training Program (SYETP). Each STEP youth participates for two summers and, during the intervening school year, participates in a variety of activities like tutoring, counseling, and social events. Since educational deficiency and teen parenting are the major causes of high school dropout, STEP's two main objectives are to improve academic skills and foster responsible social and sexual behavior. The ultimate goal is to keep participants in school through graduation.

"Dashelle was the kind of kid the teachers always forget about, the one who sits in the back and never makes any kind of contribution," says Marcia Crismond, STEP coordinator for Palm Beach. "Nobody helped her because nobody paid any attention to her. Now, no one can believe it's the same child."

Dashelle now is on the honor roll, and recently competed with her black history club in the Florida Brain Bowl. Her team placed second in the state. She now is planning on college and is actively seeking a scholarship.

STEP operates during the summer months because "we know that without some kind of educational activity going on in summer, the STEP kids are going to lose ground," says STEP Director Laurie Levin. "There's a name for it—summer learning loss."

Each STEP youth receives 90 hours of basic instruction to produce reading and math gains, or at least to decrease summer learning loss. Life Skills and Opportunities instruction teaches responsible social and sexual behavior, contraception, and the facts and consequences of teen pregnancy. Classes are active and communicative, according to Crismond. Teacher talk is minimal; students are encouraged to talk themselves. Despite her shyness, Dashelle responded well to this approach, and having the same teacher and students in her class both summers made her feel more secure.

STEP participants are paid minimum wage for both their academic activities and work at entry-level clerical, maintenance, and parks and recreation jobs.

Dashelle worked as a file clerk for Economic Services, which handles the food stamp program at the Belle Glade housing project. "They thought she was wonderful because she was not loud-mouthed," says Crismond. "They really worked with her, and she found she was capable, even around adults. They asked her back again the next summer, which made her feel fantastic."

STEP monitors students' progress during the school year to encourage attendance and make sure any gains achieved during the summer continue. In Palm Beach an advocate is available to meet each week with STEP students. And after each marking period, STEP students who have no Fs on their report cards are taken on field trips to the movies or roller skating or to Ocean World in Fort Lauderdale.

A new STEP project called Student-2-Student was introduced in January 1991 at nine pilot sites around the country. Student-2-Student was the answer for many youths like Dashelle who wanted to continue their involvement with STEP beyond 15 months. "The kids really want that sense of belonging. They are not anxious to give it up," says Levin.

Based on the theory that you learn a subject more thoroughly if you teach it, Student-2-Student is a program of peer education. It teaches interested youths, who have been through STEP's life skills training, to present some of their knowledge to other students at area schools. In the process, these "peer facilitator/educators" learn the material better themselves.

Now a peer facilitator/educator, Dashelle and a partner made two presentations to 13- and 14-year-old students in dropout prevention classes at a Palm Beach-area middle school. They put on a skit and led a class discussion about planning for the future. The message they hit home with was: "If you are concerned about being anybody in the future, you need to think about it today."

STEP research shows that its students make significant gains in math and reading after their first summer, increasing even more after their second summer. Their attendance and grades improve and many make the honor roll. STEP participants also show increased knowledge about contraception and facts related to teen pregnancy. "We continue to see gains every summer," says Levin. "I can't tell you how many times I've heard of kids who have been written off who have hit their stride, sort of gotten a toehold, with STEP."

Begun in 1984 by Public/Private Ventures (P/PV), a national nonprofit organization, STEP has grown to its current size from only five original demonstration sites. P/PV provides STEP sites with two specialized curricula, an operations manual, information and training videos, and a structured sequence of training and technical assistance at the national, state, and local on-site levels.

STEP already has served about 15,000 disadvantaged youths, and by the end of 1991 will serve another 7,000 to 8,000. The program is funded by state and local governments, the federal SYETP, and private and corporate foundations.

For more information, contact Laurie Levin, STEP Director, Public/Private Ventures, 399 Market St., Philadelphia, PA 19106, (215) 592-9099.

TAPP: Helping pregnant and parenting teens

Expectant teen fathers get a little queasy watching the birth film. "I didn't know it would be like this" is a typical response. Afterward, a parenting development specialist gives a hands-on lesson on diapering and bathing a doll. Next time, they'll use a real baby.

The young fathers are part of a discussion group for couples, one of many support groups and activities sponsored by the family service agency's Teenage Pregnancy and Parenting Project (TAPP) in San Francisco. The weekly meeting is periodically structured, but most often its young members are free to discuss whatever is on their minds with little time constraints.

"You have to provide an environment in which young people feel motivated and empowered, one that is non-punitive," says Project Manager Maryam Rashada. So over sodas, chips, and bologna sandwiches, the young people talk about anything from teen parenting to being sexually abused.

In 1981 TAPP set out to reduce low birthweight, school dropout, and the repeat birth rate among San Francisco teenagers. It has done all three. In 1989 the program received the state American Medical Association award for the project that dealt best with teen pregnancy in California.

Through continuous case management, TAPP helps pregnant and parenting teens of both sexes gain access to educational, social, health, and employment services. A continuous counselor guides each participant through whatever services will best meet his or her needs for finishing school, being a teen parent, staying healthy, having the baby stay healthy, and becoming financially self-sufficient. Mothers, fathers, and children may stay with TAPP for years, not just during the mother's pregnancy. "Continuous case working, where someone sticks with you through thick and thin, makes all the difference in the world," says Rashada.

José is a Mexican American born in the United States. At 15, he was hanging out with the wrong crowd and got a girl pregnant. It was his first sexual experience. The baby was born in 1986. The mother left the baby with José, left the state, and has not been heard from since. José and his mother have raised the child, with a lot of help from TAPP.

José, who has had the same TAPP counselor since 1986, now is finishing his second year in community college and works as a manager in a restaurant chain. Though he is 20 years old, the TAPP cutoff age for males, he has been allowed to continue informally with the program because he is so deserving.

One of TAPP's biggest challenges is to enroll teen fathers. The program places a strong emphasis on acknowledgment and establishment of paternity—not only to increase financial support for the baby, but to enable the development of a father-child relationship. Most young women will not initially reveal the father's address, however, so TAPP's community counselors are sent on "Daddy Patrol."

The object is to find the fathers, whether they are on the basketball court, aboard a bus, or in the street. To convince these young men to enroll in TAPP, counselors also must be young and male, and of similar ethnic and cultural backgrounds, says Rashada. Young black counselors work with the black fathers, Latino counselors work with Latino fathers, and Asian counselors work with the Asian fathers.

The system is good, but definitely not foolproof. One baby's father denied his paternity and ran away. The mother, a 12-year-old, gave birth to a baby boy by Caesarean section. TAPP helped put the baby in child care and learning centers so the mother could stay in school and work every summer. She and her mother—a single working parent—were determined that she would graduate. She did, in 1989, and now has finished her second year in college. The father, however, has not joined the family.

To enroll young women, TAPP's community outreach program goes wherever they are likely to be—free clinics, for example. TAPP counselors are "outstationed" at these locations with the materials necessary to enroll young women on site.

The continuous case management approach at TAPP is also used in 33 other projects in California. Together they serve 5,000 to 6,000 people a year. But that's only 6 percent of the eligible population in a state where, in 1990, 69,000 babies were born to mothers 18 and younger.

The project finished its federal funding four years ago, and since then has been depending on multi-year state contracts. While the longevity of these contracts offers a sense of security, they remain at the same level each year, regardless of inflation. So, according to Rashada, TAPP staffers try to get the most for their dollars and carefully count the pencils in the supply cabinet.

For more information, contact Charlene Clemens, project director, or Michele DuBowick, clinical supervisor, 1325 Florida Avenue, San Francisco, CA 94110, (415) 695-8300.

El Puente: Uniting body, mind, spirit, and community

Maybe you come to El Puente because you want to dance or play volleyball or learn English or play the piano. But each activity leads you down a broader path. Pretty soon you find yourself in a theater troupe that puts on 26 AIDS education programs a year, or in a project to feed the hungry.

Opened in 1983 because of community dissatisfaction with health, education, and social services, El Puente ("The Bridge") is a youth center that emphasizes individual, family, and community empowerment in five areas: health, education, achievement, personal growth, and social growth.

Orlando and Ralphie dropped out of school because their schools did not respond to the Latino culture. Both graduated from El Puente's alternative high school. Orlando started the camping program, which now is affiliated with Outward Bound and sends young people all over the country. Ralphie created the sports program, which includes a football league, volleyball, and basketball.

The young men now are in college, but both still are closely involved in the center. Orlando works at El Puente as a peer supporter, and Ralphie is the male lead in El Puente's dance ensemble.

Orlando and Ralphie's experiences at El Puente are not unique. "Young people have developed the programs according to what they need," says Luis Garden-Acosta, chief executive officer. "El Puente brings in adult specialists to consult, but the young people are the ones who really make it work. They are holistic in their focus. They create a bridge to unite the body, mind, spirit, and community."

El Puente is housed in a former Roman Catholic church on the south side of Williamsburg in Brooklyn, a neighborhood largely made up of poor and near-poor Latinos. Sixty-five percent of its residents receive some form of public assistance. The neighborhood has the highest school dropout rate for Latinos in New York City and the highest felony rate for adolescents in Brooklyn.

Inside the old church building, however, it's like a different world. The center space is open, airy, and huge. People often are sprawled on the floor painting large murals or posters to hang at El Puente or in the community. Paintings are displayed on panels along the sides of the room. Behind the panels are cubicles and desks for staff. It looks like a community center, not a social service agency.

Youths from four New York City boroughs (all except Staten Island) enroll in El Puente. Participants range in age from 12 to 21. (Those older than 21 can become volunteers or paid peer supporters.) One of the first things they do after joining is develop, with counselors, a four-month plan that incorporates their initial interests with other programs that might be interesting or beneficial. At the end of the four months, youths and staff develop a plan for continued participation.

"We are a development center," says Garden-Acosta. "We see our center as a community at large." It is the most comprehensive Latino arts center in Brooklyn, offering 26 bilingual classes in fine arts, theater, photography, and dance. In addition, a medical and fitness center, GED night school (the alternative high school no longer exists), and mental health and social services centers all are contained inside the former church.

Besides these, however, El Puente tries to provide just about whatever help its teens need. For example, many of these young people are new arrivals from the Dominican Republic or El Salvador, so one of El Puente staffers' big jobs is to help them obtain permanent resident status so they can get jobs.

Other enrollees may need help straightening out their family life. Teresa was a young teen when she joined the arts program. She was being sexually abused by a sibling, but was afraid to tell anyone. She finally told her peer supporter at El Puente. Staffers worked with her family, the District Attorney, and the Bureau of Child Welfare until the offender was removed from the household and sent to a rehabilitation center. Teresa now is an A student and a young leader in the community.

El Puente, with an annual budget of more than $1 million, is funded through state, city, and private organizations and serves about 300 young people. The program has been replicated in Chelsea and Holyoke, Massachusetts, and two other sites in New York are being developed. El Puente now is training 100 young people to staff the new programs.

For more information contact Luis Garden-Acosta, 211 South Fourth St., Brooklyn, NY 11211, (718) 387-0404.

The Door: A center for alternatives

Some aspects of The Door are easy enough to describe. It's a four-story youth center on Broome Street in New York City. It houses extensive teen health, family planning, prenatal, and well-baby care facilities; a wide range of educational services for both in-school and out-of-school youths, including a degree-granting alternative high school; counseling from job preparation to substance abuse; legal services; English as a Second Language classes; and a variety of physical, performing, creative, and martial arts programs. About 300 economically or educationally disadvantaged 12- to 21-year-olds, of various ethnic and racial groups from all over New York City, come to The Door each day. The program receives a variety of government, foundation, corporate, and individual funds.

But you can't get at what this youth center really is like without metaphors. Julie Glover, the associate director for planning and research, says The Door is "a village for teenagers," a "total education center," and "like a positive gang, with a real sense of community." The comparison that seems to work best, though, is that it's "like a shopping mall."

Like a shopping mall with its collection of stores, The Door, established in 1972, is a collection of services, community-building activities, and workshops, except everything is free. The "shopkeepers" are the staff of counselors, health care workers, teachers, job counselors, artists, and athletes who run the services and workshops. These staff members, however, are also mentors to their "shoppers." Youths who come to The Door first assess, with the help of the staff, what their interests and needs are and decide what combination of services might best meet them. As time goes by counselors and youths keeping meeting to adjust their plans. The staff members also meet daily among themselves to coordinate the care they provide to each individual teen. Young people can come to the center anytime it's open (every afternoon and evening except weekends), stay as long as they want, and use whichever services they want.

One tenth-grader attends The Door's alternative high school every day from 8:30 to 2:30 in the afternoon. At 3:00 she goes to a pottery class. An hour later she's in a counseling session. At 6:00, after dinner, she goes to a dance class. She's been coming to The Door for a year and a half now, and plans to stay until she graduates from high school.

Another young woman, a new mother who has dropped out of school, comes for GED class. While she's in class, her baby goes to the center's on-site nursery. Throughout her pregnancy this young woman came to the center for comprehensive prenatal care, including nutrition counseling and Lamaze classes. The baby now will receive free health services at The Door until age three.

No matter which individual programs or services the youths enroll in, however, they're immersed in The Door's "total person" atmosphere. Instead of focusing on pregnancy prevention or job readiness or academic achievement, The Door covers them all. Its philosophy is that young people's physical, psychological, social, intellectual, and creative needs are all inseparable and all equally important. Not only does the center accordingly offer a comprehensive range of programs and activities, but it makes a point of hiring specialists who are committed to working across disciplines.

Even the physical environment is specially designed to remove customary boundaries and bureaucracies—to look nothing like the schools and social service agencies that have frustrated or angered many of the youths The Door wants to attract. The Door is open and airy inside, with bright, warm colors everywhere. Most walls are only four or five feet high (except for enclosed rooms in the health center). The point, says Glover, is "to facilitate communication and foster a sense of connectedness."

This total dedication to the holistic approach—plus top-notch work on other fronts—has brought impressive results. The Door's GED pass rate is among New York City's highest. In one year the program placed more than 100 participants in jobs throughout the city, and Door alumni eventually have gone on to become professionals in almost every imaginable field. Youths who go through The Door's family planning programs come out several times more likely to use contraception than before. There's considerable interest among educators, social workers, and government officials in this country and abroad in replicating the program. But the holistic nature of the program—perhaps the one aspect that sets The Door apart from many other youth centers—makes it a challenge to start. One of the keys to making a program like this successful, says Glover, is "to start with all the pieces in place, even if they're small." The biggest mistake would be to start with just a job readiness component or a health component and think that the other disciplines can be added on later, she says. "Somehow you don't get around to it, or the whole program can end up dominated by the first discipline."

Fund raising for a program like The Door may be another big challenge these days, when funds typically are allocated to address specific youth problems. A program that works with youths with multiple needs must draw its funding from a variety of sources, which can make for more than the usual confusion and paperwork.

But there may be a way around that soon, if new experiments with "platform funding" prove successful. After years of negotiations, the State of New York is nearing finalization on a plan that would channel all of a program's state funds through one designated lead state agency. The first demonstration site will be The Door. Glover sees it as a "groundbreaking kind of thing. If we can do it for The Door, maybe it can be done for other places."

For more information, contact Julie Glover, The Door, 555 Broome St., New York, NY 10013, (212) 941-9090.

THE ADOLESCENT AND YOUNG ADULT FACT BOOK

Midnight Basketball League: An alternative to crime

Shootings were a fact of life when gangs controlled two public housing projects in Chicago. Crime was so rampant at the Henry Horner and Rockwell Gardens housing developments that managers could not collect rent and janitors could not clean. In early 1990 the Chicago Housing Authority offered young gang members an alternative to crime—the Midnight Basketball League (MBL).

The Chicago Housing Authority's MBL is modeled after a program begun in Prince George's County, Maryland, in 1986 as a deterrent to crime and drug activity. Most crimes were being committed there between 10:00 p.m. and 2:00 a.m. by men in their late teens and early twenties. The MBL offered those young men a positive diversion during the hours when they were most likely to get into trouble.

In Chicago, the MBL invites young men ages 18 to 25 from the Henry Horner and Rockwell Gardens projects to try out for 160 positions on 16 teams. There are eight teams from each project, and seasons last eight weeks. The year-round program mirrors the National Basketball Association (NBA) in its operation and terminology, and by providing top-quality basketball shoes, uniforms, championship rings, all-star games, and awards banquets. Though expensive, these are the hooks necessary to get the young men into the program, according to Gil Walker, Director of Sports Programs for the Chicago Housing Authority and Commissioner of the MBL.

To participate, prospective players must first fill out an application. (About 300 young men applied for the last draft.) Practices are scheduled at odd hours like 3:00 or 6:00 a.m. Those who make the practices then are allowed to try out. Attitude is more important than ability, so teams generally consist of one superstar and nine enthusiastic, mediocre-to-poor players. There always are different gang factions on each team.

"These guys used to shoot each other, but now they can't because they're on the same team...the team is their new gang," says Walker. "But this provides a family environment which these guys never had. The coaches are like surrogate fathers and the guys try to emulate them."

Basketball is only part of the MBL. The program offers discipline and responsibility often void in the lives of its participants. To stay in the league, players must follow rules barring fighting, unsportsmanlike behavior, profanity, drugs, alcohol, radios, and tape players. If they break the rules, they don't play basketball.

Practices are mandatory, as are workshops after every game. During the workshops, players are encouraged to improve themselves physically, mentally, and economically by seeking appropriate substance abuse counseling, vocational training and counseling, life skills assistance, adult education and GED services, basic health care, and various social services. Those who have been with the program two years will be required to get a GED.

"Anything they need, we try to give them," says Walker. "If they are going to a job interview and have no money, we give them a bus pass. We provide haircuts; we check their fingernails."

The program costs about $80,000 a season (eight weeks at each of the two projects where it is in place) and is funded by the Housing Authority and private donations. Like the NBA, each team has an "owner." Chicagoans who "buy" teams for $2,000 are encouraged to be hands-on owners, and frequently take players to visit their businesses and homes.

The program already has had some positive results. There still is crime at Henry Horner and Rockwell Gardens projects. There still are drive-by shootings, according to Walker, but not one man involved with the MBL has been in trouble. And "during playing time, there are no shootings. There is a truce going on."

Fifty-four of the 160 participants last year registered for adult education classes after the season ended. Forty-seven have been placed in full-time jobs, ranging from unskilled entry-level to skilled trade positions.

On his MBL application, Roosevelt Smith responded truthfully to the question: "Have you ever been in trouble before?" He wrote: "I used to rob and steal." Smith was a high school dropout, unmarried with three children. While participating in MBL, he got his GED and a plumbing certificate. He now is a plumber for a food service company and married to the mother of his children.

At an MBL awards banquet, Smith won the 1990 Role Model of the Year Award—presented to the individual who has turned his life around the most in a year. "The city went all out for us," says Walker. "All my guys were in tuxedos; limos were provided for parents. Parents said to me, 'This is the first time I've been able to cheer for my son.'"

Some MBL players are featured in "Heaven Is a Playground," a movie now being produced about an inner-city basketball league that was filmed at Chicago's Cabrini public housing development. They were paid $75 a day, and five players were sent to California to do additional shooting.

Walker also took the Chicago All-Star team to the first Midnight Basketball League national championship game in Maryland. "The thing that's so wonderful about these trips is that we're taking guys who, for the most part, society's written off, and people think they're a college team because they're so well behaved," he says.

The MBL only reaches a few of those who could most benefit from it, however. Games are, of course, open to the community, as are some workshops—100 prospective employers will participate in an upcoming open job fair. But there are 11,000 residents of the Henry Horner and Rockwell Gardens projects; about 6,600 are youths or young adults. Only 160 young men can play in the league at a time. The Housing Authority wanted to expand the MBL to other Chicago developments in 1991 but lacked the funding.

The program has been replicated in Hartford, Connecticut; Louisville, Kentucky; and Washington, D.C. Eighty-seven U.S. cities, plus Japan, Italy, and British Columbia have requested information. A major challenge, however, is to expand the program within Chicago to serve more of its own young men. Despite the praise and endorsements that the MBL has gotten from housing officials, local sports figures, and local politicians, new sources of funding have been hard to find. Housing authority officials are optimistic, though, that support will come as word of MBL's success spreads.

For more information, contact Gil Walker, MBL Commissioner, Chicago Housing Authority, 534 East 37th St., Chicago, IL 60653, (312) 791-4768.

The Children's Aid Society: Setting teens on the right path

"I'm not doing anything and I'm going nowhere," is how Miriam described herself not too long ago. She was a school dropout and a single parent with five children. When she asked her children about their homework, they would say, "What do you know?"

Now, five years after taking part in programs of the Children's Aid Society in New York City, Miriam is about to graduate from Hunter College. She was placed in an accelerated GED program. She got her GED and went on to Hunter through a special program that guarantees admission to Children's Aid Society participants who have high school diplomas or the equivalent. Now Miriam's thinking about going to law school. "You watch me look at the kids' homework now!" she says.

"People have fantastic potential if there is someone around to get them on the right pathway," says Michael Carrera, director of the Children's Aid Society's Adolescent Sexuality and Pregnancy Prevention Program.

The Children's Aid Society has three youth development centers that serve young people of Harlem's mostly black and Latino central, east, and west communities. These children frequently are from one-parent households supported entirely by some kind of public assistance. They often get their medical care from emergency rooms because they have no health insurance. The adults almost always want to work but can't find jobs. They're "a group of people falling behind in the great race," says Carrera.

It's a community with complex problems that call for complex solutions. While a primary goal of the Children's Aid Society's youth programs is reducing teen pregnancy, the program tackles much more. Carrera believes that no single intervention will influence teen behavior effectively. So the program, begun in 1985, takes a holistic approach, offering parallel but separate services for teens and their parents in seven areas: family life and sex education, counseling, education, sports, self-expression, employment, and health. "This philosophy doesn't suggest a quick fix," says Carrera. "It means hanging in there for years and years."

In 15 two-hour discussions, the family life and sex education course covers pregnancy prevention, gender roles, social roles, and intimacy. The parents' course also includes how to talk to children about sex and how to prevent child abuse.

Bolstering the family life and sex education component is the sports program, which emphasizes self-discipline and impulse control through individual mastery of sports like squash, tennis, golf, and swimming. There's also a theater program of weekly workshops with actors and actresses from Harlem's National Black Theatre. The workshops address motivation and appropriate self-expression by exploring questions ranging from "how do you express anger?" to "how do you ask a question in class?" Career awareness and job preparation classes are available through the Job Club, and all program participants receive complete physicals each year and gynecological exams and contraceptive services as needed.

To make it easier for parents to attend, child care is provided, or parents are given the money for other child care arrangements. Teen escorts are available to walk younger children or adults home after dark. And if the activity happens to be around dinner time, meals are served. "Not just Hawaiian Punch and cookies," says Carrera, "but meals prepared by people we hire for that purpose." Moreover, staff regularly remind people to come to these sessions—in person rather than by phone. "All this gives a message that we want you," says Carrera. "We don't expect them to have internal motivation. They need constant reminders. Their motivation starts to increase when their lives get better."

David always has wanted to be a pilot. Several years ago, at age 13, he came to one of the Children's Aid Society's youth development centers because he was having difficulty in school. The program helped him by providing tutoring and other essential supports while he attended the local High School of Aviation Trades.

David has been accepted by the Spartan School of Aeronautics in Oklahoma and now is applying for financial aid from various programs. The Children's Aid Society also will contribute financially. "One way or another," says Carrera, "we will provide him with what it takes to fulfill his dream. There is no question in our minds that if he wasn't involved in this kind of intensive relationship with a program where people care, this wouldn't have come about."

Funding for the program comes from the New York State Department of Social Services, foundations, corporations, and individuals. The cost per person per year is $1,500 to $1,750. The program now serves about 300 young people and 110 adults.

For more information, contact Michael Carrera, project director, The Children's Aid Society, 350 East 88th St., New York, NY 10128, (212) 876-9716.

Male Youth Project: Another route to adulthood for young black men

On the last Wednesday of each month, Shiloh Baptist Church in Washington, D.C., is loud with what sounds like a round of Jeopardy. Indeed there is a quiz game going on. But unlike the television version, the contestants here are teams of black male teenagers, and the questions are all about African American history and culture. "When is Malcolm X's birthday?" "Who was the black athlete named the NBA's Most

Valuable Player in 1991?" The prizes here also are a bit more modest than on television: the winning team gets free pizza.

The monthly African American quiz is part of Shiloh Baptist's Black Male Youth Health Enhancement Project, run by the church's Family Life Center. Usually called simply the Male Youth Project, the program was created because members and leaders of the church grew tired of seeing black boys in their community growing up without regular contact with strong, positive black men, and tired of seeing so many of their boys turn to street gangs, drugs, or violence to prove they're men.

In 1985, with a combination of private and public funding, and in joint sponsorship with the District of Columbia's Department of Human Services, Shiloh Baptist launched the Male Youth Project. The idea is to show young men that there is another way to adulthood by offering them a program of daily after-school study halls with one-on-one tutoring, weekly workshops in which teens research given topics and create relevant skits or other presentations, the monthly African American quiz, and regular conferences on black males' issues cosponsored with other community groups. The "hooks" to the project are organized sports teams and an assortment of banquets, picnics, museum visits, and movies, plus activities the youths wouldn't normally have a chance to do, like camping and skiing. For those who satisfy predetermined levels of achievement and participation, there are weekend trips— to New York, Disney World, or Myrtle Beach, for example.

The project is open to any black male between the ages of nine and 17, and all activities are led by black men from the community who also act more broadly as the young men's mentors.

The project attracts a lot of young people like Robert, one of the very first to join. Robert came only to play basketball. He wanted nothing to do with the workshops, the study halls, the conferences, or the field trips. He had trouble in school and trouble with his temper. "He was like a time bomb. He'd go off in a minute," says Gerard Bingham, the project's director. When Robert disagreed with a referee, he'd kick chairs or storm out of the gym. "We had to let him know," says Bingham, "'even though you're our best player, we can't keep you if you're like this.'" If he wanted to play, they told Robert, he had to participate in other aspects of the project, bring up his grades in school, and learn to control his temper.

Eventually, after a lot of work on the part of the project's staff and mentors, Robert began showing up at the workshops and other activities.

In the six years that have passed, Robert has grown up a lot. He's now 17 and has just "graduated" from the project. Bingham says his "attitudes and emotions" still flare up sometimes, but nothing like before. He's able to lead workshops as well as the basketball team, his grades have improved, and he's planning to go to junior college.

At the same time, the project, too, has grown up. Originally it focused strictly on health issues. Now it involves just about anything that can help black youths make the transition to adulthood. The workshops, for example, cover topics from understanding anger and anxiety to creating a small business. The program has served almost 400 youths so far, and sees an average of 35 to 45 youths each day. The project reaches well beyond Shiloh's membership to the community at large: Only 5 percent of the project's participants are Shiloh Baptist Church members.

One of the project's newest additions is a year-long "manhood training" program for 13-year-olds. The year begins with a Rites of Passage ceremony. This year 20 13-year-olds participated. After the ceremony, those who want to may begin a year of structured, individualized course of study under a mentor. The idea is to develop the body, mind, and soul through such activities as working up to a certain physical fitness goal, planning and carrying out a community service project, leading peers in discussions of current events and issues in the news, and attending a certain number of churches and other places of worship to gain a sense of the variation among different religions.

One of the biggest on-going challenges for the Male Youth Project is getting more mentors. According to Bingham, 90 percent of the young men in the project do not have fathers living with them. One day a year the project puts on a "father-son" banquet in which each young man is matched with a man from the church, who becomes the boy's father for the day. But for the rest of the year, there are only about 10 regular mentors, or one for every four or five youths. Bingham's dream is to have one mentor for each boy, and the project recently has begun to recruit men outside the church. The response so far, says Bingham, has been encouraging.

With or without the ideal number of mentors, the important thing is that the program is there every day for the community's young men, says Bingham. "If we do nothing else but have your son in our program five hours a day, then we've accomplished a lot, because that's five hours he's not on the street," he says. "You add that up, that's 25 hours a week. He may do something positive here, he may not. But the temptation to do something positive is definitely stronger here."

For more information, contact Gerard Bingham, Male Youth Project, Shiloh Family Life Center, 1510 Ninth Street, N.W., Washington, DC 20001, (202) 332-0213.

ADOLESCENTS AND YOUNG ADULTS AND THEIR FAMILIES

The 54 million adolescents and young adults (ages 10 to 24) in the United States now make up approximately one-fifth of the total population, a significantly smaller proportion than 10 years ago. Over the next few decades, the proportion will continue to decline steadily, although initially the total number in this age group will rise. By the year 2030, 10- to 24-year-olds will make up only 18 percent of the population, down from 28 percent in 1970. Blacks, Latinos, and other minorities make up an increasing proportion of this age group.

Meanwhile, the elderly population will continue to grow, closing the decades-long gap between the young and elderly populations. In 1970 teens and young adults outnumbered senior citizens three to one. By 2030 the numbers will be almost equal.

The overall population figures, however, mask large differences between racial and ethnic groups. For example, 27 percent of the Latino population are teens and young adults, as are one-third of the American Indian, Eskimo, and Aleut population. Among Asian Americans and Pacific Islanders the proportion is slightly lower than in the general population.

THE ADOLESCENT AND YOUNG ADULT FACT BOOK

The figures also vary widely within groups. For example, among Latinos, almost 30 percent of Mexican Americans are 10- to 24-year-olds, but only 17.4 percent of Cuban Americans are. Puerto Ricans and Central and South Americans fall between these two extremes: About one-fourth of each group are between the ages of 10 and 24.

Youths of different races and ethnic groups are concentrated in different parts of the country. More than half of all black children and young adults, for example, live in the South, and almost half of all Latino children and young adults live in the West. By contrast, only 8 percent of blacks live in the West, and about 7 percent of Latinos live in the Midwest.

Regardless of where in the country they live, black and Latino adolescents are concentrated in central cities, whereas white teens are concentrated in the suburbs. Almost half of all families headed by mothers live in central cities, compared with only one-fourth of all two-parent families. Almost two-thirds of all black families headed by mothers live in central cities.

Families of adolescents

Most teenagers live in two-parent families. However, living arrangements differ greatly between racial and ethnic groups. More than three-fourths of white teens and almost two-thirds of Latino teens live with two parents. On the other hand, about half of all black teens live with only one parent, usually the mother. Almost one in five black teens lives with a parent who never has married, compared with less than one in 25 Latino teens and less than one in 50 white teens. A sizable proportion of older black teens—almost 11 percent of 15- to 17-year-olds—live with neither parent.

School-age children and young adults are more likely to live in poor families now than in the late 1960s. Although most poor youths are white (because there are so many more whites than people of other races or ethnic groups), black and Latino youths are more likely to be poor. More than 40 percent of black school-age children and more than one-third of Latino school-age children are poor. About 30 percent of black and Latino young adults are poor.

There are important racial and ethnic differences in the incomes of families with teens. The median income among white families (more than $37,500 per year) is almost twice that among black families (almost $19,700 per year) and considerably higher than that among Latino families (almost

$22,300 per year). Regardless of race or Latino origin, the median income of two-parent families is two to four times that of families headed by mothers.

Parents of teenagers are most commonly between the ages of 35 and 49. However, more than one-fourth of black teens, and more than one-fourth of teens in families headed by mothers, live with a parent younger than 35. Many of these young parents were themselves teens when they became parents.

Regardless of family type, about 40 percent of both black and white adolescents have parents who graduated from high school but did not attend college. About one-fourth of all white teens have parents who graduated from college, compared with only one in 10 black teens. Almost one-third of all black teens, on the other hand, have parents who did not graduate from high school, whereas less than one in five white teens have such parents.

The story is very different for Latino teens. More than half of them, regardless of family type, have parents who either never started high school or dropped out before graduating. Less than 7 percent of Latino teens have parents who graduated from college.

More than 80 percent of adolescents have parents who are employed outside the home. The percentage is even higher for those in two-parent families. Teens with parents who are not in the labor force are disproportionately black or Latino. Families headed by mothers are especially likely to be without jobs: More than one-third of black teens in families headed by mothers, and more than 40 percent of Latino teens in such families, have parents who are not in the labor force.

Black and Latino teens are more than twice as likely as white teens to be living in rental housing. Families headed by mothers also are very likely to rent rather than own their housing. More than half of all teens in such families live in rental housing, compared with less than 18 percent of those in two-parent families. More than one in 10 adolescents in mother-headed families—almost twice the proportion in 1970—live in families doubling up with other families; they are at risk of becoming homeless.

Table 1.1

Trends in the Adolescent and Young Adult Population, by Race and Latino Origin, 1970-2030

Year	Total	White	Black	Latino*
Number (in thousands)				
1970	57,334	49,383	7,180	NA
1980	60,979	50,982	8,521	4,716
1989	53,683	43,431	8,141	5,584
2000	55,920	44,211	8,896	6,512
2030	54,138	40,532	9,360	9,599
Percent of total population				
1970	28.0%	27.5%	31.5%	NA
1980	26.8	26.1	31.7	31.9%
1989	21.6	20.7	26.4	27.2
2000	20.8	20.0	25.3	25.8
2030	18.0	17.2	21.0	22.9

*Persons of Latino origin can be of any race.
NA—Data not available.

Sources: U.S. Department of Commerce, Bureau of the Census, *Current Population Reports*, Series P-25, No. 721, Estimate of the Population of the United States by Age, Sex, and Race: 1970 to 1977 (1978), Table 1; U.S. Department of Commerce, Bureau of the Census, *Current Population Reports*, Series P-25, No. 1057, U.S. Population Estimates, by Age, Sex, Race, and Hispanic Origin: 1989 (1990), Table 1; U.S. Department of Commerce, Bureau of the Census, *Current Population Reports*, Series P-25, No. 1018, Projections of the Population of the United States, by Age, Sex, and Race: 1988 to 2080 (1989), Table 4; and U.S. Department of Commerce, Bureau of the Census, *Current Population Reports*, Series P-25, No. 995, Projections of the Hispanic Population: 1983 to 2080 (1986), Table 2. Calculations by Children's Defense Fund.

Table 1.2

Trends in the Ratio of Adolescents and Young Adults to Senior Citizens, 1970-2030

Percent of Population That Is:

Year	Adolescent, Young Adult	Elderly*	Ratio
1970	28.0%	9.8%	2.9:1
1980	26.8	11.3	2.4:1
1989	21.6	12.5	1.7:1
2000	20.8	13.0	1.6:1
2030	18.0	17.9	1.0:1

*Age 65 and older.

Sources: U.S. Department of Commerce, Bureau of the Census, *Current Population Reports*, Series P-25, No. 721, Estimates of the Population of the United States by Age, Sex, and Race: 1970 to 1977 (1978), Table 1; U.S. Department of Commerce, Bureau of the Census, *Current Population Reports*, Series P-25, No. 1057, U.S. Population Estimates, by Age, Sex, Race, and Hispanic Origin: 1989 (1990), Table 1; U.S. Department of Commerce, Bureau of the Census, *Current Population Reports*, Series P-25, No. 1018, Projections of the Population of the United States, by Age, Sex, and Race: 1988 to 2080 (1989), Table 4; and U.S. Department of Commerce, Bureau of the Census, *Current Population Reports*, Series P-25, No. 995, Projections of the Hispanic Population: 1983 to 2080 (1986), Table 2. Calculations by Children's Defense Fund.

Table 1.3

Adolescent and Young Adult Population, by Race and Age, 1989 (Numbers in Thousands)

Age	Total	White	Black	Other*
10-14	16,950	13,574	2,679	696
15-19	17,847	14,367	2,767	713
15-17	10,169	8,123	1,623	423
18-19	7,678	6,245	1,144	290
20-24	18,886	15,490	2,695	701
Total, ages 10-24	53,683	43,431	8,141	2,110
10- to 24-year-olds as percent of total population	21.6%	20.7%	26.4%	24.4%

*Includes Asians, Pacific Islanders, American Indians, Alaskan Natives, and Aleuts.

Source: U.S. Department of Commerce, Bureau of the Census, *Current Population Reports*, Series P-25, No. 1057, U.S. Population Estimates, By Age, Sex, Race, and Hispanic Origin: 1989 (1990), Table 1. Calculations by Children's Defense Fund.

Table 1.4

Latino Adolescent and Young Adult Population, by Latino Subgroup and Age, 1989 (Numbers in Thousands)

Latino Subgroup

Age	All Latino	Mexican	Puerto Rican	Cuban	Central, South American	Other Latino
10-14	1,835	1,325	204	50	148	108
15-19	1,726	1,158	192	63	218	95
20-24	1,893	1,232	193	73	274	121
Total, ages 10-24	5,454	3,715	589	186	640	324
10- to 24-year-olds as percent of total population	27.2%	29.6%	25.3%	17.4%	25.2%	20.7%

Source: U.S. Department of Commerce, Bureau of the Census, unpublished tabulations from the March 1989 Current Population Survey. Calculations by Children's Defense Fund.

Fig. 1.1

Adolescents and Young Adults Ages 10 to 24 As a Percent of the Population, by Race and Latino Subgroup, 1989

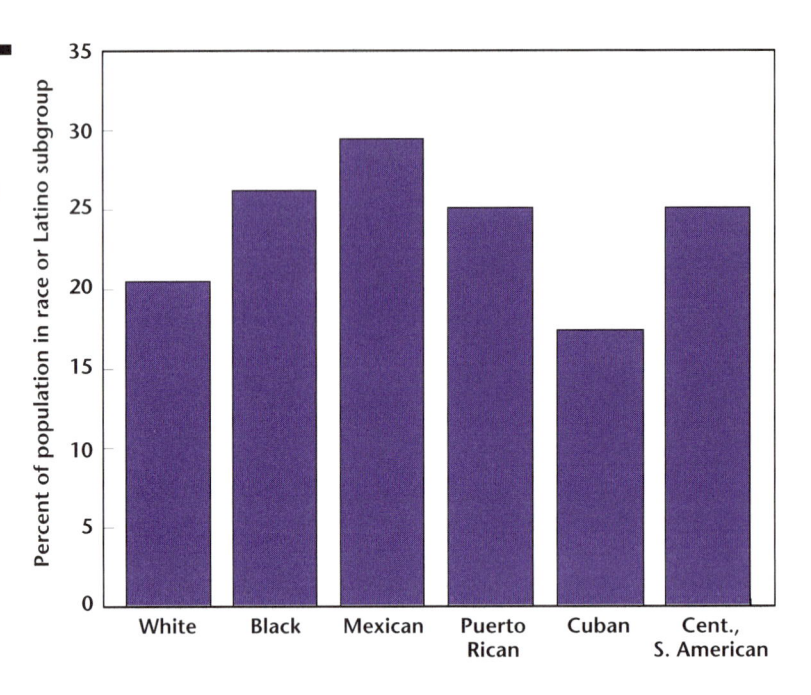

Group	Percent
White	~20.5
Black	~26
Mexican	~29.5
Puerto Rican	~25
Cuban	~17.5
Cent., S. American	~25

Source: Tables 1.3 and 1.4.

Table 1.5

Adolescent and Young Adult Population, Races Other Than Black and White, by Race and Age, 1980

Age	American Indian, Eskimo, and Aleut	Asian and Pacific Islander
10-14	163,835	298,010
15-19	180,904	304,702
20-24	162,985	339,874
Total, ages 10-24	507,724	942,586
10- to 24-year-olds as percent of total population	33.1%	25.3%
Ratio of adolescent to elderly population	6.4:1	4.3:1

Source: U.S. Department of Commerce, Bureau of the Census, *1980 Census of Population*, Volume 1, Characteristics of the Population, Chapter C, General Social and Economic Characteristics, Part 1, United States Summary (1983), Table 120. Calculations by Children's Defense Fund.

Table 1.6

Regional Distribution of School-Age Children and Young Adults, by Race and Latino Origin and by Age, 1990 (Percent in Each Region)

Age, Region	Total	White	Black	Latino*
Ages 6-17				
Northeast	19.1%	19.6%	16.8%	13.9%
Midwest	24.6	25.9	21.2	6.7
South	34.4	31.4	53.7	31.3
West	21.9	23.2	8.3	48.1
Ages 18-24				
Northeast	20.0	20.6	16.8	16.0
Midwest	24.9	26.1	21.4	7.8
South	34.0	31.5	53.8	27.9
West	21.1	21.8	8.0	48.2

*Persons of Latino origin can be of any race.

Source: U.S. Department of Commerce, Bureau of the Census, unpublished tabulations from the March 1990 Current Population Survey. Calculations by Children's Defense Fund.

Table 1.7

Residential Distribution of Families with Adolescents Ages 12 to 17, by Race and Latino Origin and Family Type, 1989 (Percent)

Family Type, Residence	Total	White	Black	Latino*
All families				
Central city	28.4%	22.8%	56.8%	50.8%
Non-metropolitan area	24.0	25.7	17.0	8.7
Two-parent families				
Central city	23.5	20.4	47.7	47.1
Non-metropolitan area	25.4	26.6	19.9	9.8
Mother-headed families				
Central city	44.5	33.8	64.8	59.6
Non-metropolitan area	19.4	22.2	14.9	6.5

*Persons of Latino origin can be of any race.

Source: U.S. Department of Commerce, Bureau of the Census, *Current Population Reports*, Series P-20, No. 445, Marital Status and Living Arrangements: March 1989 (1990), Table 6. Calculations by Children's Defense Fund.

Fig. 1.2

Percent of Families With Adolescents Ages 12 to 17 Living in Central Cities, by Family Type and Race and Latino Origin, 1989

*Persons of Latino origin can be of any race.

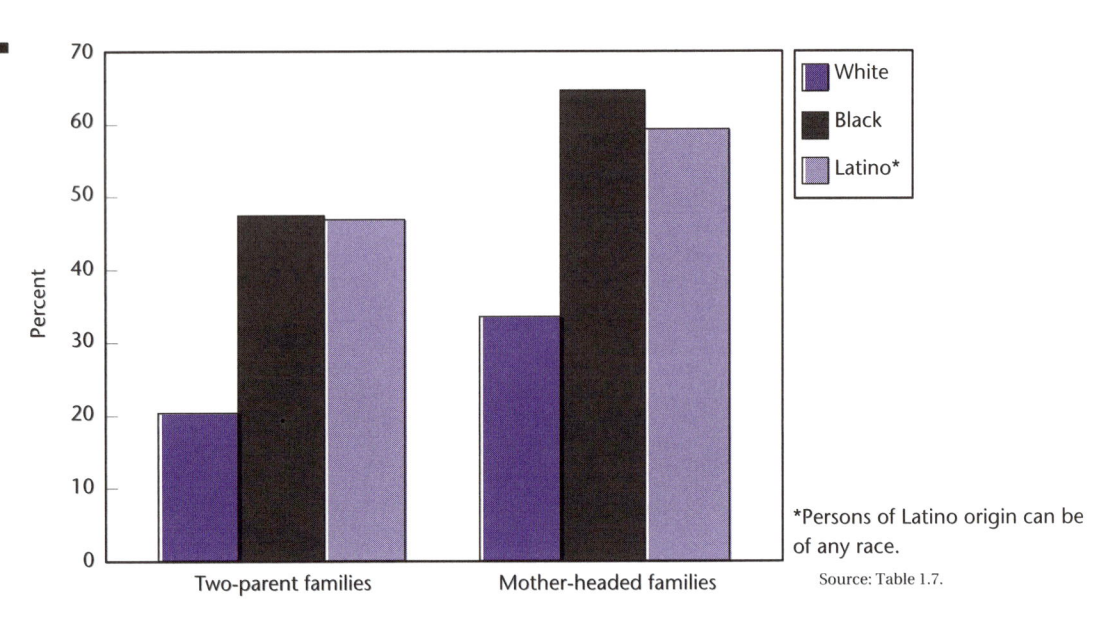

Source: Table 1.7.

Table 1.8

Living Arrangements of Adolescents Ages 10 to 17, by Race and Latino Origin and Age, 1989 (Percent)

Age, Living Arrangement	Total	White	Black	Latino*
10-14				
Living with two parents	72.8%	78.5%	41.9%	67.7%
Living with one parent	24.8	20.0	50.7	29.9
Living with mother only	21.6	16.8	47.3	26.8
Living with father only	3.2	3.2	3.3	3.1
Living with neither parent	2.4	1.5	7.5	2.4
15-17				
Living with two parents	70.6	76.2	40.8	63.1
Living with one parent	24.8	20.5	48.4	31.2
Living with mother only	21.4	16.9	45.2	27.4
Living with father only	3.4	3.5	3.2	3.9
Living with neither parent	4.5	3.2	10.7	5.6

*Persons of Latino origin can be of any race.

Source: U.S. Department of Commerce, Bureau of the Census, *Current Population Reports*, Series P-20, No. 445, Marital Status and Living Arrangements: March 1989 (1990), Tables 4 and 5. Calculations by Children's Defense Fund.

Table 1.9

Trends in Percent of Adolescents Ages 10 to 17 Living With One Parent Only, by Race and Latino Origin, 1970-1989 (Percent)

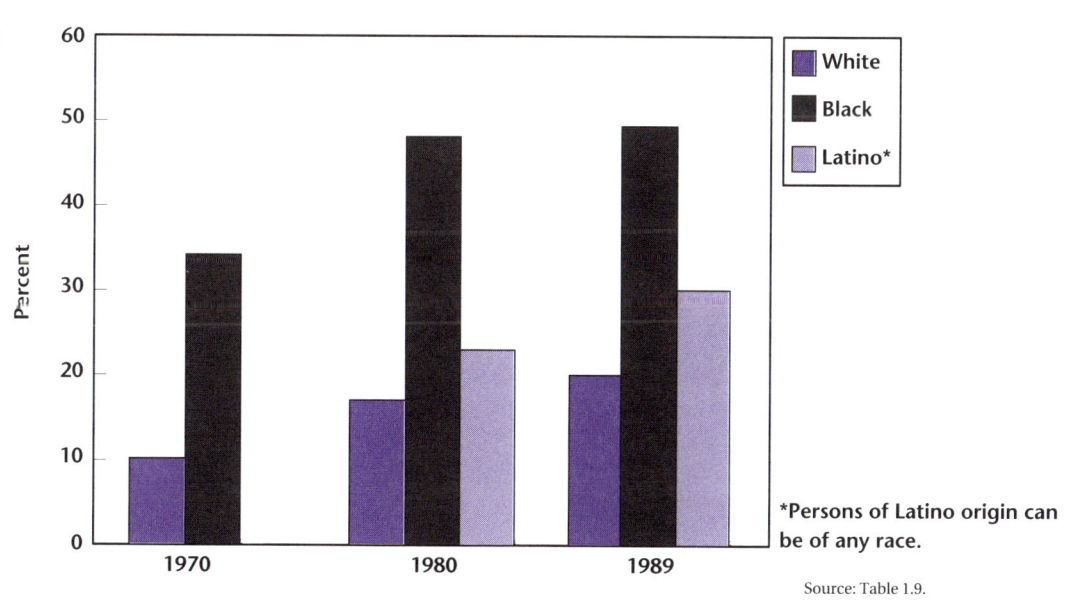

Living Arrangement, Year	Total	White	Black	Latino*
Living with one parent				
1970	13.2%	10.0%	34.6%	NA
1980	21.4	16.8	48.2	23.1%
1989	24.8	20.2	49.8	30.4
Living with one parent, parent never married				
1970	0.5	0.1	2.8	NA
1980	1.6	0.5	8.0	2.8
1989	4.2	1.5	18.5	4.8
Of those living with one parent, percent whose parent never married				
1970	3.6	1.2	8.1	NA
1980	7.3	2.7	16.5	12.0
1989	16.8	7.6	37.1	15.7

*Persons of Latino origin can be of any race.
NA — Data not available.

Source: U.S. Department of Commerce, Bureau of the Census, *Current Population Reports*, Series P-20, No. 212, Marital Status and Family Status: March 1970 (1971), Tables 4 and 5; U.S. Department of Commerce, Bureau of the Census, *Current Population Reports*, Series P-20, No. 365, Marital Status and Living Arrangements: March 1980 (1981), Tables 4 and 5; and U.S. Department of Commerce, Bureau of the Census, *Current Population Reports*, Series P-20, No. 445, Marital Status and Living Arrangements: March 1989 (1990), Tables 4 and 5. Calculations by Children's Defense Fund.

Fig. 1.3

Trends in Percent of Adolescents Ages 10 to 17 Living With One Parent Only, by Race and Latino Origin, 1970-1989

*Persons of Latino origin can be of any race.

Source: Table 1.9.

THE ADOLESCENT AND YOUNG ADULT FACT BOOK

Table 1.10

Trends in the Poverty Rate Among School-Age Children and Young Adults, by Race and Latino Origin and by Age, 1969-1989 (Percent Below Poverty Level)

Age, Year	Total	White	Black	Latino*
6-15				
1969	14.1%	10.0%	39.3%	NA
1974	15.7	11.2	42.1	NA
1979	15.9	11.6	39.5	27.8%
1984	20.7	15.8	45.8	39.0
1989	18.6	14.0	41.3	34.6
16-21				
1969	11.7	8.9	29.6	NA
1974	12.3	8.9	34.7	NA
1979	12.6	9.1	34.6	21.3
1984	17.5	14.1	35.5	31.5
1989	15.3	12.0	31.7	28.5

*Persons of Latino origin can be of any race.
NA— Data not available.

Sources: U.S. Department of Commerce, Bureau of the Census, *Current Population Reports*, Series P-60, No. 76, 24 Million Americans: Poverty in the United States: 1969 (1970), Table 4; U.S. Department of Commerce, Bureau of the Census, *Current Population Reports*, Series P-60, No. 102, Characteristics of the Population Below the Poverty Level: 1974 (1976), Table 6; U.S. Department of Commerce, Bureau of the Census, *Current Population Reports*, Series P-60, No. 125, Money Income and Poverty Status of Families and Persons in the United States: 1979 (Advance Report) (1980), Table 20; U.S. Department of Commerce, Bureau of the Census, *Current Population Reports*, Series P-60, No. 149, Money Income and Poverty Status of Families and Persons in the United States: 1984 (Advance Data From the March 1985 Current Population Survey) (1985), Table 17; and U.S. Department of Commerce, Bureau of the Census, *Current Population Reports*, Series P-60, No. 168, Money Income and Poverty Status in the United States: 1989 (Advance Data From the March 1990 Current Population Survey) (1990), Table 22. Calculations by Children's Defense

Table 1.11

Distribution of Family Income Among Families with Adolescents Ages 12 to 17, by Race and Latino Origin, 1989 (Percent)

Family Type, Family Income	Total	White	Black	Latino*
All families				
Under $10,000	11.1%	7.8%	28.5%	19.5%
$10,000-$19,999	15.3	13.9	22.1	25.2
$20,000-$49,999	44.9	46.6	36.4	41.8
$50,000 +	28.7	31.8	12.9	13.4
Median income	$34,880	$37,541	$19,673	$22,272
Two-parent families				
Under $10,000	3.8%	3.0%	7.6%	8.3%
$10,000-$19,999	10.1	10.0	11.1	23.6
$20,000-$49,999	48.9	48.3	55.0	50.2
$50,000 +	37.2	38.8	26.4	17.8
Median income	$42,111	$43,143	$38,717	$27,575
Mother-headed families				
Under $10,000	34.8%	28.5%	48.4%	47.9%
$10,000-$19,999	32.0	31.0	31.6	28.8
$20,000-$49,999	29.9	36.6	18.5	19.9
$50,000 +	3.3	4.0	1.4	3.7
Median income	$13,902	$16,400	$10,358	$10,443

*Persons of Latino origin can be of any race.

Source: U.S. Department of Commerce, Bureau of the Census, *Current Population Reports*, Series P-20, No. 445, Marital Status and Living Arrangements: March 1989 (1990), Table 6. Calculations by Children's Defense Fund.

Table 1.12

Adolescents Ages 12 to 17, by Race and Latino Origin, Family Type, and Age of Parent, 1989 (Percent)

Family Type, Age of Parent	Total	White	Black	Latino*
All families				
15-34	12.3%	10.2%	25.9%	16.9%
35-49	75.2	77.2	64.4	70.4
50 +	12.5	12.5	9.8	12.7
Two-parent families				
15-34	8.6	8.4	13.5	14.7
35-49	77.1	77.8	71.9	70.8
50 +	14.3	13.7	14.6	14.5
Mother-headed families				
15-34	25.1	19.5	37.7	22.6
35-49	68.9	73.9	57.7	69.8
50 +	6.0	6.5	4.4	7.4

*Persons of Latino origin can be of any race.

Source: U.S. Department of Commerce, Bureau of the Census, *Current Population Reports*, Series P-20, No. 445, Marital Status and Living Arrangements: March 1989 (1990), Table 6. Calculations by Children's Defense Fund.

Table 1.13

Adolescents Ages 12 to 17, by Race and Latino Origin, Family Type, and Education of Parent, 1989 (Percent)

Family Type, Education of Parent	Total	White	Black	Latino*
All families				
No high school	9.2%	8.8%	9.4%	37.7%
Some high school	11.8	9.8	22.9	16.1
High school graduate, no college	38.2	38.1	41.1	25.8
Some college	18.8	19.5	16.5	13.7
College graduate	22.0	23.7	10.2	6.7
Two-parent families				
No high school	8.8	8.4	10.6	37.5
Some high school	9.1	8.2	17.5	14.0
High school graduate, no college	37.4	37.5	40.6	26.9
Some college	19.0	19.5	17.1	13.5
College graduate	25.6	26.4	14.2	8.2
Mother-headed families				
No high school	9.6	9.9	7.8	36.2
Some high school	20.6	16.7	28.3	22.1
High school graduate, no college	40.9	41.3	41.5	24.1
Some college	17.9	19.6	15.3	13.7
College graduate	11.0	12.4	7.1	3.9

*Persons of Latino origin can be of any race.

Source: U.S. Department of Commerce, Bureau of the Census, *Current Population Reports*, Series P-20, No. 445, Marital Status and Living Arrangements: March 1989 (1990), Table 6. Calculations by Children's Defense Fund.

Fig. 1.4

Percent of Adolescents Ages 12 to 17 Whose Parent Is Not a High School Graduate, by Family Type and Race and Latino Origin, 1989

*Persons of Latino origin can be of any race.

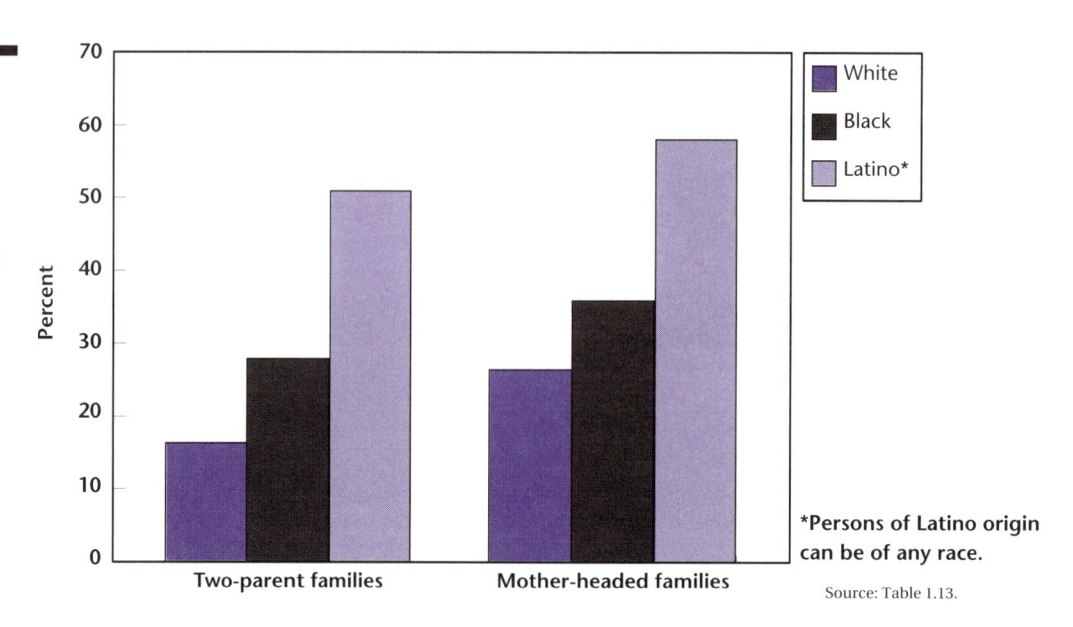

Source: Table 1.13.

Table 1.14

Adolescents Ages 12 to 17, by Race and Latino Origin, Family Type, and Parental Employment Status, 1989 (Percent)

Family Type, Parental Employment	Total	White	Black	Latino*
All families				
Employed	83.5%	86.6%	67.8%	74.9%
Unemployed	4.0	3.4	7.7	4.8
Not in labor force	11.3	9.0	23.1	19.4
Two-parent families				
Employed	89.0	90.3	80.3	84.0
Unemployed	3.2	2.9	4.9	4.5
Not in labor force	6.2	5.5	11.7	10.4
Mother-headed families				
Employed	65.3	70.6	55.7	51.4
Unemployed	6.6	5.2	9.7	5.9
Not in labor force	28.1	24.2	34.5	42.5

*Persons of Latino origin can be of any race.

Source: U.S. Department of Commerce, Bureau of the Census, *Current Population Reports*, Series P-20, No. 445, Marital Status and Living Arrangements: March 1989 (1990), Table 6. Calculations by Children's Defense Fund.

Table 1.15

Housing Arrangements of Families With Adolescents Ages 12 to 17, by Race and Latino Origin and Family Type, 1989 (Percent)

Family Type, Housing Arrangement	Total	White	Black	Latino*
All families				
Own	72.2%	77.8%	44.3%	52.8%
Rent	27.8	22.2	55.7	47.2
Public	4.3	2.4	15.1	7.3
Private	23.5	19.8	40.6	39.9
Two-parent families				
Own	82.3	84.6	67.5	63.4
Rent	17.7	15.4	32.6	36.6
Public	1.1	0.7	4.4	2.6
Private	16.6	14.7	28.2	34.1
Mother-headed families				
Own	40.1	49.1	22.7	29.7
Rent	60.0	50.9	77.3	70.1
Public	14.5	9.3	25.4	17.4
Private	45.4	41.6	51.9	52.7

*Persons of Latino origin can be of any race.

Source: U.S. Department of Commerce, Bureau of the Census, *Current Population Reports*, Series P-20, No. 445, Marital Status and Living Arrangements: March 1989 (1990), Table 6. Calculations by Children's Defense Fund.

Table 1.16

Trends in Percent of Adolescents Living in Doubled-Up Families, by Race and Latino Origin and Family Type, 1970-1988 (Percent)

Family Type, Year	Total	White	Black	Latino*
Two-parent families				
1970	0.4%	0.3%	1.0%	NA
1980	0.5	0.4	0.6	0.7%
1989	0.8	0.7	1.1	1.0
Mother-headed families				
1970	5.4	4.9	6.5	NA
1980	6.4	7.3	4.4	6.9
1989	10.0	10.3	10.2	6.9

*Persons of Latino origin can be of any race.
NA — Data not available.

Sources: U.S. Department of Commerce, Bureau of the Census, *Current Population Reports*, Series P-20, No. 212, Marital Status and Family Status: March 1970 (1971), Table 4; U.S. Department of Commerce, Bureau of the Census, *Current Population Reports*, Series P-20, No. 365, Marital Status and Living Arrangements: March 1980 (1981), Table 4; and U.S. Department of Commerce, Bureau of the Census, *Current Population Reports*, Series P-20, No. 445, Marital Status and Living Arrangements: March 1989 (1990), Table 4. Calculations by Children's Defense Fund.

HEALTH

Adolescents and young adults generally are characterized as healthy and strong. But in addition to routine illnesses and injuries, teens and young adults are subject to special health problems relating to growth and development as well as to risk-taking behavior. For many young people, poor health results from the accumulated effects of inadequate health care throughout childhood.

Health status, illness, and disability

Poverty greatly affects the health of school-age children and young adults. Poor five- to 24-year-olds are much more likely than their nonpoor peers to describe themselves or be described by their parents as having fair or poor health. Hardest hit in this age group are poor black and Latina females ages 18 to 24, who are six to eight times more likely to be in fair or poor health than their nonpoor white male peers.

Disability also is more likely among both poor adolescents and young adults, who are about 50 percent more likely than their nonpoor age peers to have a physical or mental impairment. In 1988, there were almost 2 million disabled adolescents and 1.4 million disabled young adults in the United States. Among 10- to 18-year-olds, disabilities most often result from mental disorders, including psychoses, substance abuse, and mental retardation. Among 19- to 24-year-olds, however, diseases of the musculoskeletal system, such as arthritis and noncongenital limb deformities (which may be caused by accidents), are the leading cause of impairment. For both age groups, the likelihood of disability decreases as the education of the parent or head of household increases.

Adolescents and young adults are particularly vulnerable to certain sexually transmitted diseases, especially gonorrhea and syphilis. The incidence of these diseases among youths is three to four times that in the general population. In 1989 there were almost 450,000 new cases of gonorrhea among teens and young adults, more than half of all new cases in the country. There were 15,000 new cases of syphilis in this age group, more than one-third of the total for the nation. Other diseases, such as measles and mumps, often considered only childhood illnesses, in fact also strike older adolescents, whose immunizations may be inadequate. The incidence of measles among older teens is more than three times the rate of the general population. More than one-third of all the measles cases reported in 1989 were among adolescents.

Mortality

Since 1960 overall death rates have declined significantly among 10- to 14-year-olds and somewhat among older youths and young adults. Homicide and suicide rates, however, have increased dramatically, more than doubling among 10- to 24-year-olds, and now are the second and third leading causes of death among 15- to 24-year-olds. The leading cause of death for this age group as well as younger adolescents remains motor vehicle accidents. Together, all violent deaths — accidents, homicide, and suicide — account for more than three-fourths of all deaths among youths.

Gender and racial differences figure prominently in these figures. Males are far more likely to die from violent causes than females; black youths are much more likely to die from homicide than white youths, whereas suicide is more common among white youths. Deaths from motor vehicle accidents also occur more frequently among white youths. Firearm deaths, whether homicide, suicide, or accident, are a major cause of death, particularly among black male adolescents and young adults.

Utilization of health care

Many children and youths go without health care for long periods of time. The problem may be greatest for adolescents: In 1988 about half of all eight- to 17-year-olds had not received preventive health care in the previous year. Additionally, poor school-age children are less likely than their nonpoor peers to have seen a physician in the past two years. And, just as they are more likely than whites or blacks to be completely uninsured, Latino teens are more likely to lack a regular source of health care.

Poverty also is a strong factor when it comes to the utilization of dental care. Relatively large numbers of poor school-age children have never seen a dentist, and even more have not seen a dentist in more than two years. By comparison, nonpoor school-age children are much more likely to have adequate dental care.

The gap is less pronounced for 18- to 24-year-olds, who are much less likely than younger youths to have seen a dentist in the past two years, regardless of whether they are poor.

Access to health care

In 1988, according to the National Health Interview Survey, 5.8 million eight- through 17-year-olds were completely uninsured, a major barrier to regular health care. As might be expected, youths in the worst health are the least likely to be insured.

Poverty is a major determinant of insurance status. Poor 10- to 18-year-olds are more than three times more likely than their nonpoor peers to lack coverage. Although the gap is less dramatic among 19- to 24-year-olds, income levels remain an important factor.

Age and race also play important roles. Young adults as a whole are almost twice as likely as teens to lack health insurance, and Latino youths, regardless of age, are much more likely than black or white youths to be completely uninsured. Although white and black 12- to 14-year-olds had similar rates of uninsuredness in 1988, the white children were more likely to be covered by private insurance through a parent's employment and black children were more likely to be eligible for Medicaid coverage. As a result, as black children grow up and lose their Medicaid eligibility, the proportion who are uninsured rises, while it remains essentially stable for white children.

Fig. 2.1

Perceived Health Status of School-Age Children and Young Adults, by Age, Gender, and Poverty Status, 1988

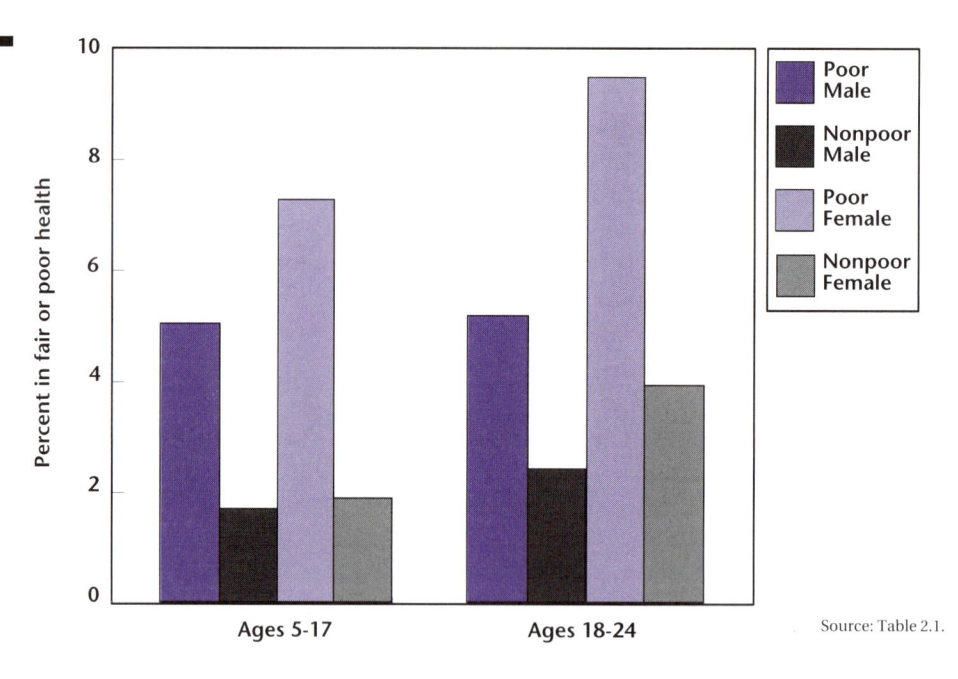

Source: Table 2.1.

Table 2.1

Perceived Health Status by Race and Latino Origin, Age, Gender, and Poverty Status, 1988 (Percent in Fair or Poor Health)

Age, Gender, Poverty Status	Total	White	Black	Latino*
Ages 5-17				
Male				
Poor	5.0%	4.1%	7.0%	4.2%
Nonpoor	1.7	1.5	3.0	2.9
Female				
Poor	7.3	6.4	8.7	6.6
Nonpoor	1.9	1.8	2.6	3.2
Ages 18-24				
Male				
Poor	5.2	4.0	7.9	4.5
Nonpoor	2.4	2.1	3.2	4.3
Female				
Poor	9.5	8.6	13.4	15.7
Nonpoor	3.9	3.8	3.8	4.5

*Persons of Latino origin can be of any race.

Source: National Center for Health Statistics, unpublished data from the 1988 National Health Interview Survey. Calculations by Children's Defense Fund.

Table 2.2

Rates for Selected Notifiable Diseases Among Adolescents and Young Adults, by Age, 1989 (Cases per 100,000 Population in Age Group)

Disease	10-14	Age 15-19	20-24
Measles	13.0	24.7	8.4
Rubella	0.1	0.1	0.2
Mumps	0.6	1.1	0.6
AIDS	0.2	0.6	7.4
Gonorrhea	69.7	1,145.4	1,204.1
Syphilis	1.3	24.7	56.1
Tuberculosis	1.2	2.9	6.6

Source: Centers for Disease Control, *Morbidity and Mortality Weekly Report*, Vol. 38, No. 54, Summary of Notifiable Diseases, United States: 1989 (October 5, 1990), pp. 10-11. Calculations by Children's Defense Fund.

Table 2.3

Trends in Rates for Selected Notifiable Diseases, 1950-1989 (Cases per 100,000 Total Population)

Disease	1950	1960	1970	1980	1989
Measles	211.0	245.4	23.2	6.0	7.3
Rubella	NA*	NA*	27.8	1.7	0.2
Mumps	NA*	NA*	55.6	3.9	2.3
AIDS	NA+	NA+	NA+	NA+	13.6
Gonorrhea	192.5	145.3	297.2	445.0	295.3
Syphilis	16.7	9.1	11.0	12.1	17.9
Tuberculosis	80.5	30.8	18.2	12.3	9.5

NA— Data not available.

*Rubella and mumps were not reportable diseases in 1950 and 1960.

+AIDS was not identified as a disease until after 1980.

Source: National Center for Health Statistics, *Health United States: 1988* (March 1989), Table 39; and Centers for Disease Control, *Morbidity and Mortality Weekly Report*, Vol. 38, No. 54, Summary of Notifiable Diseases, United States: 1989 (October 5, 1990), pp. 10-11. Calculations by Children's Defense Fund.

Table 2.4

Prevalence of Disability Among Adolescents and Young Adults, by Age and by Various Characteristics, 1984 (Percent with Disability)

Characteristic	Age 10-14	Age 19-24
Gender		
Male	7.2%	6.2%
Female	5.2	5.2
Race and ethnicity		
White, non-Latino	6.2	5.9
Black, non-Latino	6.2	5.3
Latino	6.7	4.4
Poverty status		
Poor	8.6	8.5
Nonpoor	5.9	5.1
Education of parent or head of household		
No high school	9.7	7.8
Some high school	8.2	6.7
High school graduate, no college	6.2	5.7
Some college	5.4	5.4
College graduate	5.1	4.8

Source: Paul W. Newacheck, Adolescents with Special Health Needs: Prevalence, Severity, and Access to Health Services, *Pediatrics*, Vol. 84, No. 5 (November 1989), Table 3; and Margaret A. McManus, Paul W. Newacheck, and Ann M. Greaney, Young Adults with Special Health Care Needs: Prevalence, Severity, and Access to Health Services, *Pediatrics*, Vol. 86, No. 5 (November 1990), Table 3.

Table 2.5

Leading Causes of Disability Among Adolescents and Young Adults, by Age, 1984 (Numbers in Thousands)

Cause	Ages 10-18 Number	Ages 10-18 Percent*	Ages 19-24 Number	Ages 19-24 Percent*
All causes	1,979		1,390	
Mental disorders	634	32.0%	169	12.2%
Diseases of the respiratory system	406	20.5	153	11.0
Diseases of the musculo-skeletal system and connective tissue	295	14.9	524	37.7
Diseases of the nervous system	115	5.8	133	9.6
Diseases of the ear and mastoid process	80	4.0	57	4.1

*Percent of all causes of disability.

Source: Paul W. Newacheck, Adolescents with Special Health Needs: Prevalence, Severity, and Access to Health Services, *Pediatrics*, Vol. 84, No. 5 (November 1989), Tables 1 and 2; and Margaret A. McManus, Paul W. Newacheck, and Ann M. Greaney, Young Adults with Special Health Care Needs: Prevalence, Severity, and Access to Health Services, *Pediatrics*, Vol. 86, No. 5 (November 1990), Tables 1 and 2.

Table 2.6

Trends in Adolescent and Young Adult Death Rates, by Selected Causes and Age, 1960-1988 (Deaths per 100,000 Population in Age Group)

Cause, Year	10-14	Age 15-19	20-24
All causes			
1960	44.0	92.2	123.6
1970	40.6	110.3	148.0
1980	30.8	97.9	132.7
1988	27.5	88.0	115.4
Malignancies			
1960	6.1	7.7	9.0
1970	5.2	7.3	9.4
1980	3.9	5.4	7.2
1988	3.1	4.4	5.7
Cardiovascular diseases			
1960	2.6	4.9	9.0
1970	1.8	3.9	6.2
1980	1.4	3.1	5.1
1988	1.4	2.8	4.8
Influenza and pneumonia			
1960	2.0	2.8	3.2
1970	1.5	2.1	2.8
1980	0.5	0.6	1.0
1988	0.4	0.5	0.9
Accidents			
1960	18.8	50.7	62.5
1970	20.3	63.9	74.2
1980	15.3	57.9	65.4
1988	12.7	46.7	52.2
Suicide			
1960	0.5	3.6	7.1
1970	0.6	5.9	12.2
1980	0.8	8.5	16.1
1988	1.4	11.3	15.0
Homicide			
1960	0.5	4.0	8.2
1970	1.2	8.1	16.0
1980	1.4	10.6	20.6
1988	1.7	11.7	19.0

Source: Public Health Service, *Vital Statistics of the United States: 1960, Vol. II—Mortality, Part A* (1963), Table 5-12; National Center for Health Statistics, *Vital Statistics of the United States: 1970, Volume II—Mortality, Part A* (1974), Table 1-8; National Center for Health Statistics, *Vital Statistics of the United States: 1980, Volume II—Mortality, Part A* (1974), Table 1-8; and National Center for Health Statistics, *Vital Statistics of the United States: 1988, Volume II—Mortality, Part A* (1974), Table 1-9.

Table 2.7

Leading Causes of Death Among Adolescents and Young Adults, Ages 15 to 24, 1988 (Deaths per 100,000 Population Ages 15-24)

Cause	Rate
All Causes	102.1
Motor vehicle accidents	38.5
Homicide	15.4
Suicide	13.2
All other accidents	11.0
Malignancies	5.1
Diseases of the heart	2.9
AIDS	1.4
Congenital anomalies	1.3
Cerebrovascular diseases	0.7
Pneumonia and influenza	0.7
All other causes	11.9

Source: National Center for Health Statistics, *Monthly Vital Statistics Report*, Vol. 39, No. 7, Supplement, Advance Report of Final Mortality Statistics, 1988 (November 28, 1990), Table 7.

Table 2.8

Firearm Death Rates Among Adolescents and Young Adults, by Race, Gender, and Age, 1988 (Deaths per 100,000 Population in Specified Group)

Gender, Age	White	Black
Male		
10-14	4.2	7.8
15-19	21.7	79.5
20-24	29.8	119.2
Female		
10-14	1.1	3.6
15-19	3.8	8.4
20-24	4.5	13.9

Source: National Center for Health Statistics, *Monthly Vital Statistics Report*, Vol. 39, No. 11, Supplement, Firearm Mortality Among Children, Youth, and Young Adults 1-34 Years of Age, Trends and Current Status: United States, 1979-88 (March 14, 1991), Table 1.

Fig. 2.2

Firearm Death Rates Among Adolescent and Young Adult Males, by Age and Race, 1988

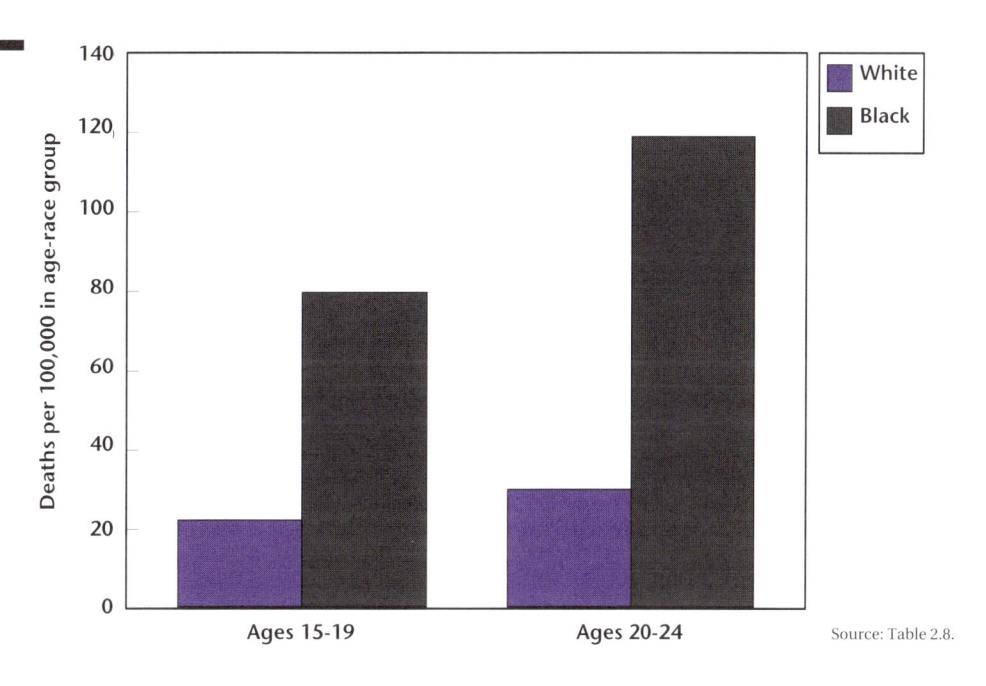

Source: Table 2.8.

Fig. 2.3

Homicide Death Rates Among Adolescent and Young Adult Males, by Age and Race, 1988

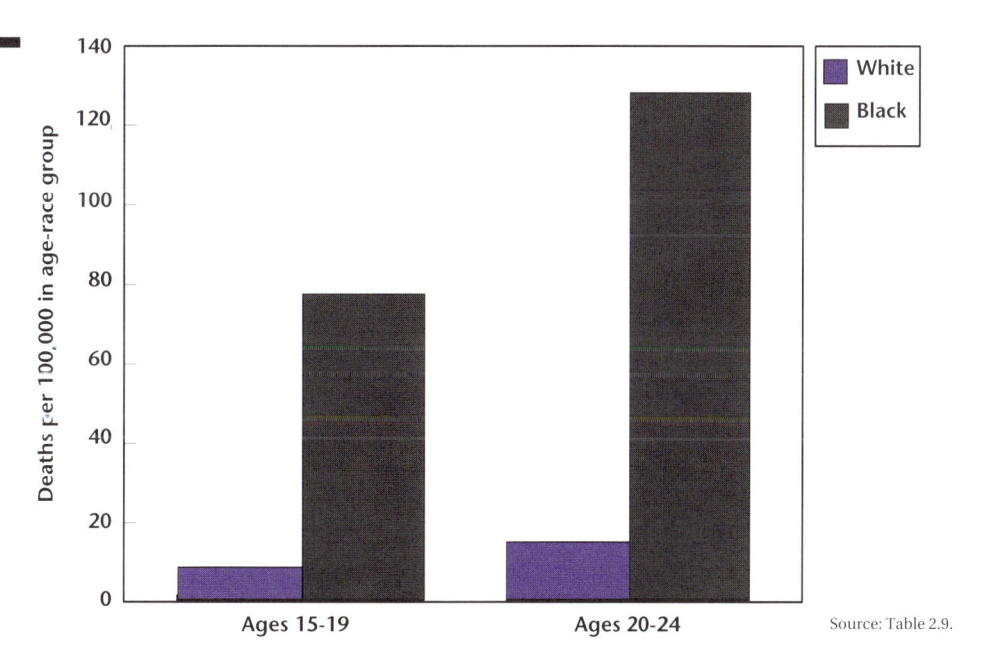

Source: Table 2.9.

THE ADOLESCENT AND YOUNG ADULT FACT BOOK

Table 2.9

Homicide Death Rates Among Adolescents and Young Adults, by Race, Gender, and Age, 1988 (Deaths per 100,000 Population in Specified Group)

Gender, Age	Total	White	Black
Male			
10-14	2.0	1.3	5.7
15-19	18.8	8.1	77.4
20-24	30.4	14.8	128.2
Female			
10-14	1.4	0.8	4.4
15-19	4.4	3.0	11.5
20-24	7.4	4.7	23.3

Source: National Center for Health Statistics, *Vital Statistics of the United States: 1988, Vol. II—Mortality, Part A* (1991), Table 1-9.

Table 2.10

Suicide Death Rates Among Adolescents and Young Adults, by Race, Gender, and Age, 1988 (Deaths per 100,000 Population in Specified Group)

Gender, Age	Total	White	Black
Male			
10-14	2.1	2.1	1.3
15-19	18.0	19.6	9.7
20-24	25.8	27.0	19.8
Female			
10-14	0.8	0.8	0.9
15-19	4.4	4.8	2.2
20-24	4.1	4.4	2.9

Source: National Center for Health Statistics, *Vital Statistics of the United States: 1988, Vol. II—Mortality, Part A* (1991), Table 1-9.

Fig. 2.4

Suicide Death Rates Among Adolescents and Young Adults, by Age, Race, and Gender, 1988

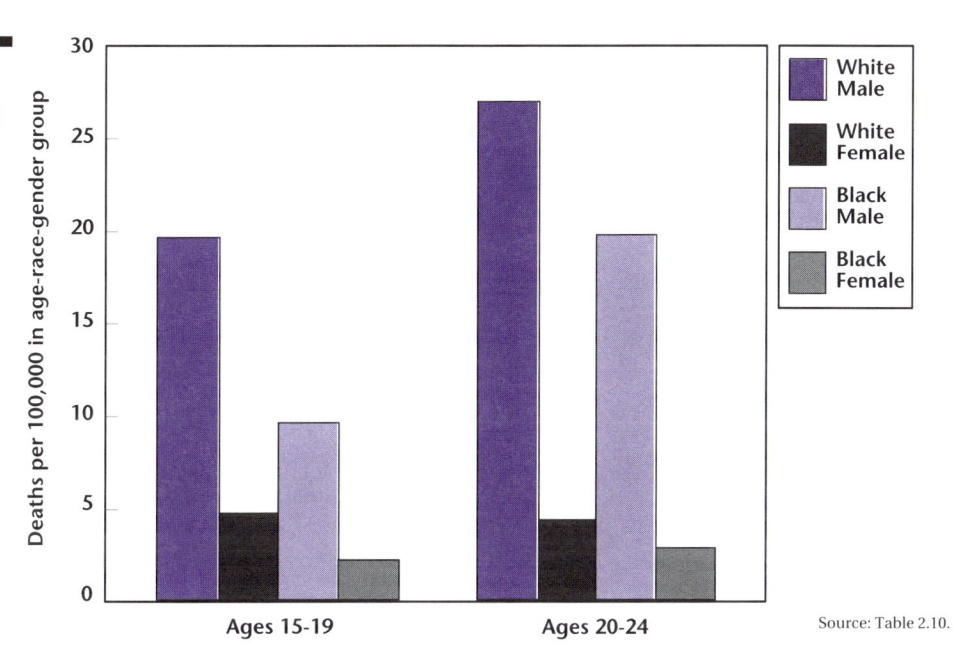

Source: Table 2.10.

Table 2.11

Accident Death Rates Among Adolescents and Young Adults, by Race, Gender, and Age, 1988 (Deaths per 100,000 Population in Specified Group)

Gender, Age	Total	White	Black
Male			
10-14	17.0	16.6	19.8
15-19	67.1	71.8	45.9
20-24	82.9	84.8	72.5
Female			
10-14	8.2	7.8	9.6
15-19	25.4	28.0	12.5
20-24	21.4	22.0	17.4

Source: National Center for Health Statistics, *Vital Statistics of the United States: 1988, Vol. II—Mortality, Part A* (1991), Table 1-9.

Table 2.12

Motor Vehicle Accident Death Rates Among Adolescents and Young Adults, by Race, Gender, and Age, 1988 (Deaths per 100,000 Population in Specified Group)

Gender, Age	Total	White	Black
Male			
10-14	9.4	9.8	8.5
15-19	51.3	56.3	28.9
20-24	61.6	64.1	47.7
Female			
10-14	5.5	5.6	4.6
15-19	22.6	25.2	9.9
20-24	17.7	18.8	11.5

Source: National Center for Health Statistics, *Vital Statistics of the United States: 1988, Vol. II—Mortality, Part A* (1991), Table 1-9.

Fig. 2.5

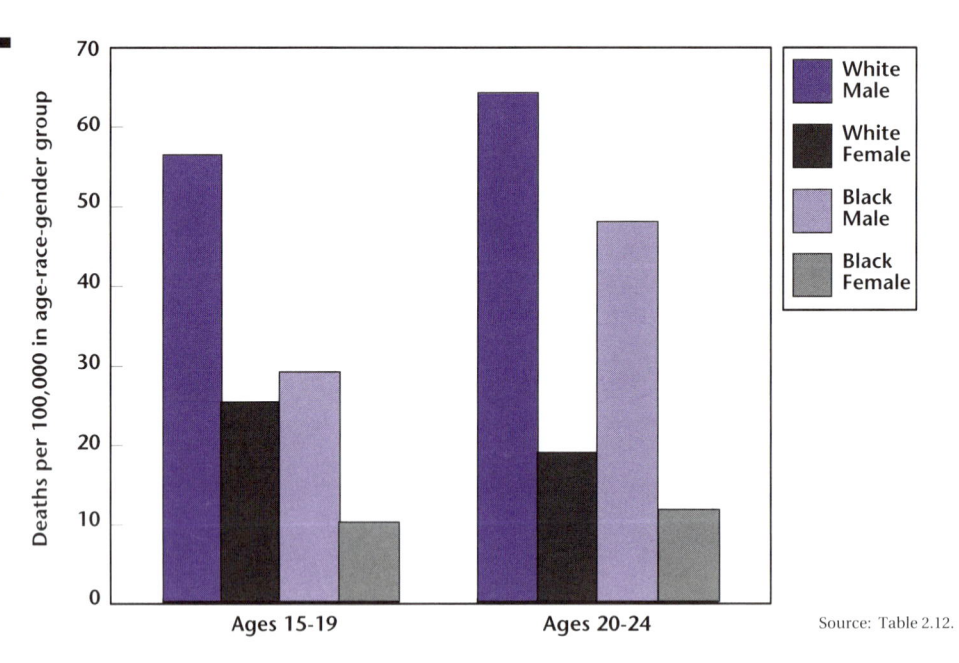

Motor Vehicle Accident Death Rates Among Adolescents and Young Adults, by Race, Gender, and Age, 1988

Source: Table 2.12.

Table 2.13

Recency of Physician Visit, by Race and Latino Origin, Age, and Poverty Status, 1988 (Percent)

Age, Recency of Visit, Poverty Status	Total	White	Black	Latino*
Ages 5-17				
Never visited a doctor				
Poor	0.5%	0.7%	0.2%	1.4%
Nonpoor	0.1	0.1	0.2	0.4
No visit in past two years				
Poor	13.5	14.3	11.9	15.4
Nonpoor	9.6	9.3	11.2	13.7
Ages 18-24				
Never visited a doctor				
Poor	0.3	0.4	0.0	2.2
Nonpoor	0.2	0.1	0.2	0.5
No visit in past two years				
Poor	11.5	11.1	10.7	22.2
Nonpoor	14.6	14.1	17.6	19.5

*Persons of Latino origin can be of any race.

Source: National Center for Health Statistics, unpublished data from the 1988 National Health Interview Survey. Calculations by Children's Defense Fund.

Table 2.14

Recency of Dental Visit, by Race and Latino Origin, Age, and Poverty Status, 1986 (Percent)

Age, Recency of Visit, Poverty Status	Total	White	Black	Latino*
Ages 5-17				
Never visited a dentist				
Poor	14.5%	14.6%	13.9%	21.9%
Nonpoor	5.7	5.3	9.4	11.6
No visit in past two years				
Poor	19.1	17.9	21.4	18.9
Nonpoor	10.1	9.5	15.5	14.2
Ages 18-24				
Never visited a dentist				
Poor	4.2	2.6	9.1	7.6
Nonpoor	1.7	1.3	4.0	5.0
No visit in past two years				
Poor	29.4	25.7	40.1	33.1
Nonpoor	25.2	23.8	34.6	33.2

*Persons of Latino origin can be of any race.

Source: National Center for Health Statistics, unpublished data from the 1986 National Health Interview Survey. Calculations by Children's Defense Fund.

Table 2.15

Adolescents Not Receiving Routine Health Care, by Race and Latino Origin and by Age, 1988 (Percent not Receiving Routine Health Care in Past Year)

Age	Total	White	Black	Latino*
8-11	50.4%	52.1%	44.3%	50.5%
12-14	45.2	44.0	48.3	48.1
15-17	46.1	46.0	44.3	54.5

*Persons of Latino origin can be of any race.

Source: National Center for Health Statistics, *Advance Data*, Number 188, Health Insurance and Medical Care: Health of Our Nation's Children, United States, 1988 (October 1, 1990), Table 2. Calculations by Children's Defense Fund.

Table 2.16

Adolescents With No Regular Source of Health Care, by Race and Latino Origin and by Age, 1988 (Percent with No Regular Source of Health Care)

Age	Total	White	Black	Latino*
8-11	13.1%	12.8%	13.6%	18.4%
12-14	15.0	14.9	13.8	27.4
15-17	17.1	16.6	17.1	27.8

*Persons of Latino origin can be of any race.

Source: National Center for Health Statistics, *Advance Data*, Number 188, Health Insurance and Medical Care: Health of Our Nation's Children, United States, 1988 (October 1, 1990), Table 3. Calculations by Children's Defense Fund.

Table 2.17

Health Insurance Coverage of Adolescents and Young Adults, by Age and Various Characteristics, 1984 (Percent with No Coverage)

Characteristic	Age 10-18	Age 19-24
Gender		
Male	14.5%	29.5%
Female	13.8	23.4
Race and ethnicity		
White, non-Latino	11.1	22.7
Black, non-Latino	18.1	34.2
Latino	29.8	44.2
Poverty status		
Poor	30.9	36.4
Nonpoor	9.4	22.3
Living arrangements		
With both parents	11.4	NA
With one parent	18.9	NA
With other relatives	34.7	NA

NA— Data not available.

Source: Paul W. Newacheck and Margaret A. McManus, Health Insurance Status of Adolescents in the United States, *Pediatrics*, Vol. 84, No. 4 (October 1989), Table 2; and Margaret A. McManus, Ann M. Greaney, and Paul W. Newacheck, Health Insurance Status of Young Adults in the United States, *Pediatrics*, Vol. 84, No. 4 (October 1989), Table 1.

Table 2.18

Health Insurance Coverage of Adolescents and Young Adults, by Age and Perceived Health Status, 1984 (Percent with No Coverage)

Perceived Health Status	Age 10-18	Age 19-24
Excellent	10.8%	23.1%
Very good	13.0	24.4
Good	22.5	33.0
Fair or poor	24.6	36.4

Source: Paul W. Newacheck and Margaret A. McManus, Health Insurance Status of Adolescents in the United States, *Pediatrics*, Vol. 84, No. 4 (October 1989), Table 4; and Margaret A. McManus, Ann M. Greaney, and Paul W. Newacheck, Health Insurance Status of Young Adults in the United States, *Pediatrics*, Vol. 84, No. 4 (October 1989), Table 3.

Table 2.19

Health Insurance Coverage of Adolescents and Young Adults, by Race and Latino Origin and by Age, 1988 (Percent with No Coverage)

Age	Total	White	Black	Latino*
8-11	16.2%	16.4%	15.9%	35.0%
12-14	17.0	16.3	18.3	31.9
15-17	17.7	16.5	22.4	31.7

*Persons of Latino origin can be of any race.

Source: National Center for Health Statistics, *Advance Data*, Number 188, Health Insurance and Medical Care: Health of Our Nation's Children, United States, 1988 (October 1, 1990), Table 1. Calculations by Children's Defense Fund.

Fig. 2.6

Health Insurance Status of Adolescents, by Race and Latino Origin, 1988

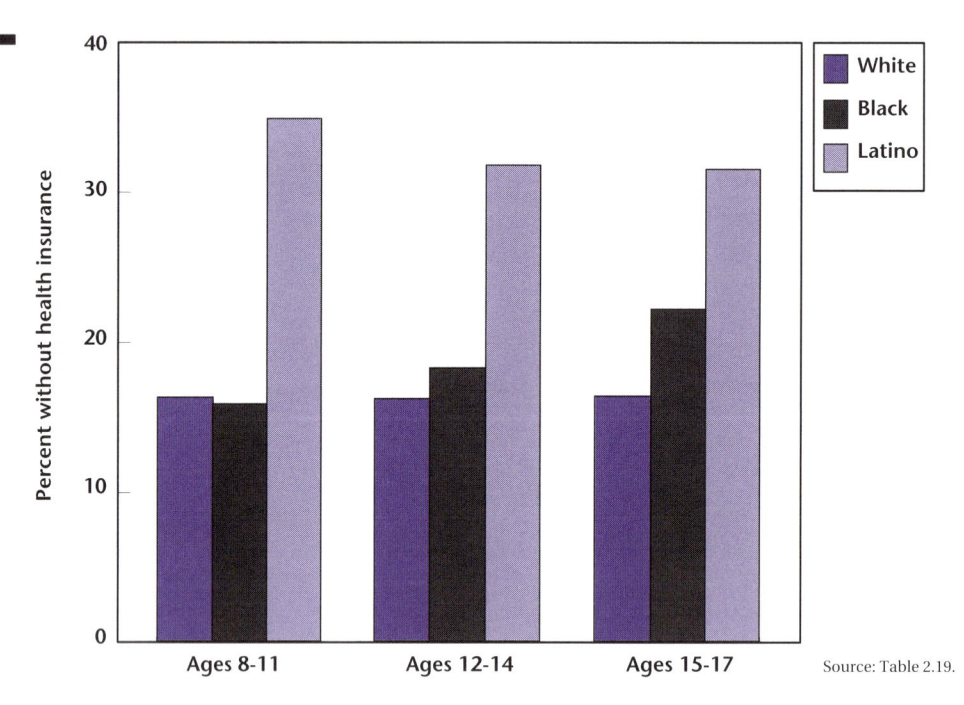

Source: Table 2.19.

CHILDREN'S DEFENSE FUND

SUBSTANCE ABUSE, CRIME, AND VICTIMIZATION

On a pleasant July evening, as Marcia Williams drove her three children toward home on a busy Washington, D.C. thoroughfare, a shoot-out erupted between two nearby cars. Her children, ages three, eight, and nine, saw their 27-year-old mother killed by a stray bullet—another victim in what police say is a war between young men involved in rival drug gangs.

America has a drug crisis evident in such violence, in young lives ruined by addiction and substance-related crime, and in the thousands of babies born damaged by alcohol, crack cocaine, and other drugs.

Most adults probably can point to something in their youth—a nurturing family, a church or synagogue, a good school, or a supportive neighborhood—that helped them make the successful transition to adulthood. But too many of today's teenagers have no such basic supports. Left to their own immature judgment and negative peer pressure, and sometimes burdened by unmet physical or emotional needs, many youths stray into drug and alcohol abuse and crime, a lifestyle that too often ends in jail or even violent death.

The destruction hits hardest among youths in many inner cities and poor neighborhoods—youths who are often black or Latino. In 1988 the firearm death rate for males ages 15 to 19 reached an all-time high of 18 per 100,000, a 43 percent increase since 1984. America is failing its teenagers. Here is the evidence.

Substance abuse

By their late teens, more than 60 percent of American youths call themselves "current" drinkers. More than one-third are smokers, one in seven uses marijuana, and about one in 25 uses cocaine, including crack. The average teenage smoker starts smoking before age 12, and teenage drinkers start drinking at about age 13.

Incredible as it may seem, these and other data represent a decline in alcohol and other drug use among young people in the past few years. Most notably, the proportion of 12- to 25-year-olds who currently use illicit drugs (drugs other than alcohol and tobacco) has dropped by about half since 1985, according to the National Household Survey on Drug Abuse.

Still, in 1990 almost one-fourth of all 12- to 17-year-olds and more than half of all 18- to 25-year-olds surveyed reported having used illicit drugs some time in their lives. A large percentage—between about 8 and 19 percent, depending on age and gender—said they used drugs within the past month.

These figures may be a conservative estimate, since the survey does not include youths who may be particularly vulnerable to substance abuse, such as the homeless; those in jails, prisons, juvenile detention, and long-term health care facilities; and college students living in dormitories.

Among all youths who say they ever have used drugs, Latinos and white non-Latinos are most likely to be frequent users. Contrary to what some may believe, black youths are less likely to use crack than either Latinos or white non-Latinos. Among adults ages 26 to 34, however, crack use among blacks is higher than the other groups, and more than twice as high as among younger blacks. Similarly, studies of infants born exposed to drugs, including crack, show that the average age of the mother is in the mid- to late twenties.

Having definite, positive plans for the future seems to make a significant difference in teens' use of illicit drugs. High school seniors who plan to graduate from a four-year college are less likely to have used drugs than those with other post-high school plans.

That's not the case with alcohol, however. Use of alcohol, the most frequently used substance among teens and young adults, is equally common among seniors with and without plans to graduate from four-year colleges.

Alcohol use also is particularly common among whites and males. In 1988 more than half of all nationally surveyed males ages 12 to 17, and more than 90 percent of males ages

18 to 25, said they had used alcohol some time in their lives. About one-fourth of the younger group and three-fourths of the older group said they had a drink in the past month.

More than one in 10 in the older group also is a heavy drinker, defined as having at least five drinks per occasion on five or more days in the previous month. Even more common are daily drinking and binge drinking (five or more drinks in a row in the past two weeks) among high school seniors.

Crime

Since 1981 the arrest rate for drunk driving among teenagers has declined, in part because the legal drinking age has been raised to 21 in all states, and in part because of increased public education against drinking and driving targeted at young people. Nonetheless young people still are much more likely than the general public to be arrested for drunk driving.

Other types of crimes also remain a serious problem among youths. The arrest rate for drug offenses increased 15-fold between 1965 and 1975 and has decreased only somewhat since then. Since 1965 the arrest rate among 18-year-olds for weapons violations has climbed steadily, and the arrest rates for violent crime and property crime have about doubled, although most of the increase was before 1975.

The data show a strong link between crime and alcohol or illegal drugs. More than half of all young people incarcerated for criminal acts used alcohol or illegal drugs regularly before imprisonment. Almost one-third were under the influence of alcohol when they committed their most recent offense, and about 40 percent were under the influence of illegal drugs.

There also are racial and family patterns. According to the U.S. Department of Justice, the majority of children held in public juvenile detention, correctional, and shelter facilities (including both delinquents and children who have not committed offenses, such as runaways) in 1985 were white. By 1989 the racial mix had shifted dramatically, with black and Latino children making up the majority.

Despite the stereotype, most incarcerated young offenders are white, due to the size of the white population. However, black youths also are more likely to be incarcerated than whites. More than half of all youths incarcerated for criminal acts lived in one-parent families when they were children, primarily with their mothers.

Regardless of the type of crime, young males are more likely to be arrested than females. Almost all males in public juvenile facilities are held for delinquent acts, such as property offenses, probation violations, other public order offenses, and alcohol and drug offenses. In contrast, almost one-fourth of females are held for reasons other than delinquency, primarily status offenses such as running away and truancy.

Victimization

Violence is the leading cause of death among American teens and young adults, especially black males. Black males ages 10 to 24 are about two to four times more likely, depending on age, than their white peers to be victims of handgun crime. They also are two to four times more likely to be killed by firearms involved in homicides, suicides, or accidents.

White youths, on the other hand, are much more likely to be victims of theft. Regardless of race or whether the crime is theft or a violent offense, females generally are less likely to be victimized than males.

Child abuse and neglect, another form of victimization among teens, often is overlooked and thought to affect only young children. In fact physical, sexual, and emotional abuse, and educational neglect (keeping children out of school) all increase with age. Teenage girls are the most likely victims of sexual abuse.

A small though significant number of teens try to escape abuse by running away from home. A recent national survey found that girls are more likely to run away than boys, and that of all runaways nationwide, two-thirds are 16 or 17 years old. Many teens are "thrownaways"—forced out of their homes, abandoned, or deserted by their parents. Almost 85 percent of these children are 16 or 17 years old.

Table 3.1

Trends in the Use of Illicit Drugs Among Adolescents and Young Adults, by Gender and Age, 1985-1990 (Percent Using Any Illicit Drug)

When Used, Gender, Age	1985	1988	1990
Ever used			
Male			
12-17	31.3%	23.7%	23.4%
18-25	66.5	58.8	59.4
Female			
12-17	27.7	25.7	22.0
18-25	63.1	59.1	52.3
Used in past month			
Male			
12-17	16.6	9.5	8.6
18-25	30.0	21.8	18.9
Female			
12-17	13.4	8.9	7.6
18-25	21.0	14.1	11.0

Note: These data are from the 1985, 1988, and 1990 Household Surveys on Drug Abuse. Excluded from the surveys are persons in institutions (jails, prisons, juvenile detention facilities, long-term care health facilities), students in college dormitories, members of the military, and the homeless. Drug use among some of these groups is higher than it is among the general population. Hence the estimates of drug use in this table are conservative.

Sources: U.S. Department of Health and Human Services, National Institute on Drug Abuse, *National Household Survey on Drug Abuse: Population Estimates 1985* (1987), Table 14-A; U.S. Department of Health and Human Services, National Institute on Drug Abuse, *National Household Survey on Drug Abuse: Population Estimates 1988* (1989), Table 2-A; and U.S. Department of Health and Human Services, National Institute on Drug Abuse, *National Household Survey on Drug Abuse: Population Estimates 1990* (1991), Table 2-A.

Table 3.2

Marijuana Use by Adolescents and Young Adults, by Race and Latino Origin, Gender, and Age, 1988 (Percent Using)

When Used, Gender, Age	Total	White Non-Latino	Black Non-Latino	Latino
Ever used				
Male				
12-17	16.8%	16.9%	15.2%	16.5%
18-25	56.4	58.2	52.5	48.0
Female				
12-17	17.9	19.4	11.8	17.2
18-25	56.4	62.5	39.1	35.7
Used in past month				
Male				
12-17	6.1	6.0	4.3	5.4
18-25	20.0	20.0	21.1	18.9
Female				
12-17	6.7	7.6	4.4	4.9
18-25	11.2	11.6	9.8	8.6

Note: These data are from the 1988 Household Survey on Drug Abuse. Excluded from the survey are persons in institutions (jails, prisons, juvenile detention facilities, long-term care health facilities), students in college dormitories, members of the military, and the homeless. Drug use among some of these groups is higher than it is among the general population. Hence the estimates of drug use in this table are conservative.

Source: U.S. Department of Health and Human Services, National Institute on Drug Abuse, *National Household Survey on Drug Abuse: Main Findings 1988* (1990), Tables 3.1, 3.3, and 3.5.

Fig. 3.1

Current Marijuana Use by Adolescents and Young Adults, by Race and Latino Origin, Gender, and Age, 1988

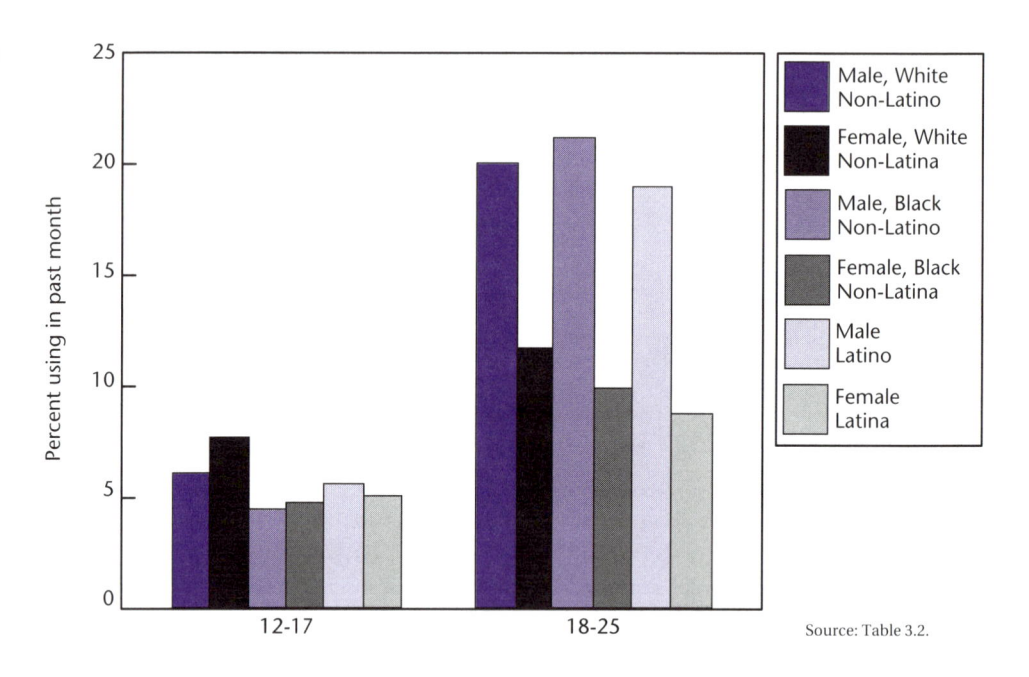

Source: Table 3.2.

Table 3.3

Cocaine Use by Adolescents and Young Adults, by Race and Latino Origin, Gender, and Age, 1988 (Percent Using)

When Used, Gender, Age	Total	White Non-Latino	Black Non-Latino	Latino
Ever used				
Male				
12-17	3.3%	3.4%	2.2%	5.2%
18-25	22.2	23.1	13.3	23.0
Female				
12-17	3.4	3.8	2.0	4.0
18-25	17.4	19.5	7.9	14.3
Used in past month				
Male				
12-17	0.9	0.9	—	1.2
18-25	6.0	5.5	6.8	10.0
Female				
12-17	1.4	1.7	—	—
18-25	3.0	2.9	2.2	—

— Number too small to calculate a reliable rate.

Note: These data are from the 1988 Household Survey on Drug Abuse. Excluded from the survey are persons in institutions (jails, prisons, juvenile detention facilities, long-term care health facilities), students in college dormitories, members of the military, and the homeless. Drug use among some of these groups is higher than it is among the general population. Hence the estimates of drug use in this table are conservative.

Source: U.S. Department of Health and Human Services, National Institute on Drug Abuse, *National Household Survey on Drug Abuse: Main Findings 1988* (1990), Tables 4.1, 4.3, and 4.5.

Table 3.4

Crack Use by Adolescents and Young Adults, by Race and Latino Origin, and Age, 1988 (Percent Using)

When Used, Gender, Age	Total	White Non-Latino	Black Non-Latino	Latino
Ever used				
12-17	0.9%	0.9%	0.8%	1.3%
18-25	3.4	3.3	2.8	5.4
Used in past year				
12-17	0.7	0.7	—	0.9
18-25	1.9	1.7	—	3.5

— Number too small to calculate a reliable rate.

Note: These data are from the 1988 Household Survey on Drug Abuse. Excluded from the survey are persons in institutions (jails, prisons, juvenile detention facilities, long-term care health facilities), students in college dormitories, members of the military, and the homeless. Drug use among some of these groups is higher than it is among the general population. Hence the estimates of drug use in this table are conservative.

Source: U.S. Department of Health and Human Services, National Institute on Drug Abuse, *National Household Survey on Drug Abuse: Main Findings 1988* (1990), Tables 4.8 and 4.9.

Table 3.5

Alcohol Use by Adolescents and Young Adults, by Race and Latino Origin, Gender, and Age, 1988 (Percent Using)

When Used, Gender, Age	Total	White Non-Latino	Black Non-Latino	Latino
Ever used				
Male				
12-17	53.4%	57.7%	38.5%	44.8%
18-25	91.6	93.3	82.5	88.6
Female				
12-17	46.8	49.4	34.6	49.4
18-25	89.1	93.5	76.5	77.6
Used in past month				
Male				
12-17	26.8	28.7	19.7	26.1
18-25	74.5	77.2	57.3	74.8
Female				
12-17	23.5	25.9	12.1	24.7
18-25	56.6	60.7	43.8	47.6

Note: These data are from the 1988 Household Survey on Drug Abuse. Excluded from the survey are persons in institutions (jails, prisons, juvenile detention facilities, long-term care health facilities), students in college dormitories, members of the military, and the homeless. Drug use among some of these groups is higher than it is among the general population. Hence the estimates of drug use in this table are conservative.

Source: U.S. Department of Health and Human Services, National Institute on Drug Abuse, *National Household Survey on Drug Abuse: Main Findings 1988* (1990), Tables 7.1, 7.3, and 7.5.

Fig. 3.2

Current Alcohol Use by Adolescents and Young Adults, by Race and Latino Origin, Gender, and Age, 1988

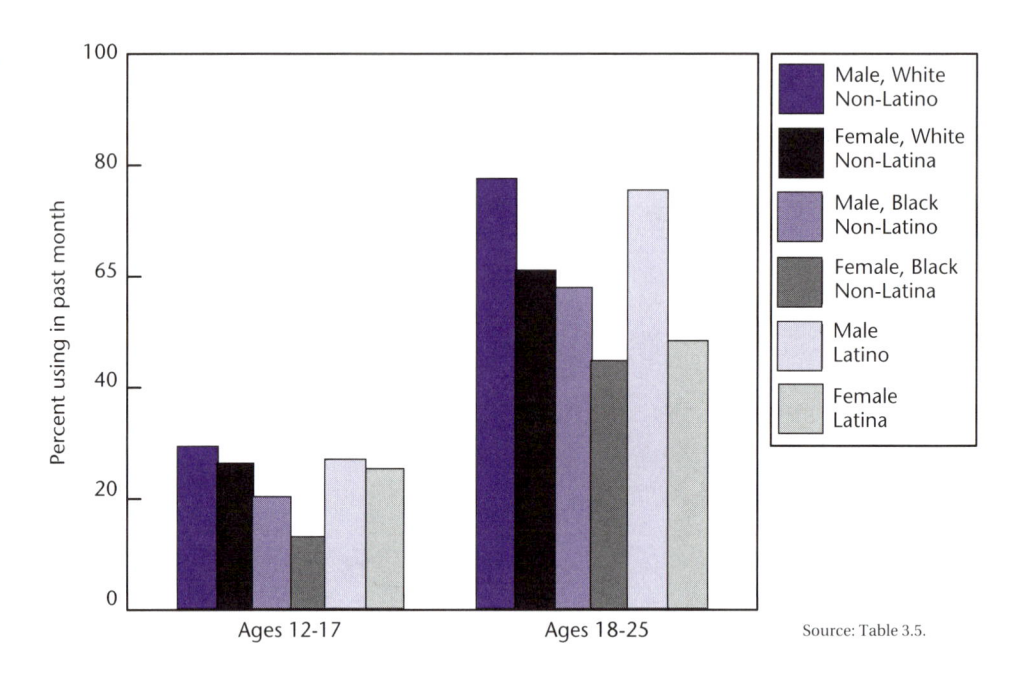

Legend:
- Male, White Non-Latino
- Female, White Non-Latina
- Male, Black Non-Latino
- Female, Black Non-Latina
- Male Latino
- Female Latina

Y-axis: Percent using in past month (0-100)
X-axis: Ages 12-17, Ages 18-25

Source: Table 3.5.

Table 3.6

Heavy Alcohol Use* by Adolescents and Young Adults, by Race and Latino Origin, and Age, 1988 (Percent)

Age	Total	White Non-Latino	Black Non-Latino	Latino
12-17	2.3%	2.8%	—	2.5%
18-25	10.3	11.0	6.5%	9.1

*Five or more drinks per occasion on five or more days in past month.
— Number too small to calculate a reliable rate.

Note: These data are from the 1988 Household Survey on Drug Abuse. Excluded from the survey are persons in institutions (jails, prisons, juvenile detention facilities, long-term care health facilities), students in college dormitories, members of the military, and the homeless. Drug use among some of these groups is higher than it is among the general population. Hence the estimates of drug use in this table are conservative.

Source: U.S. Department of Health and Human Services, National Institute on Drug Abuse, *National Household Survey on Drug Abuse: Main Findings 1988* (1990), Table 7.7.

Table 3.7

Cigarette Use by Adolescents and Young Adults, by Race and Latino Origin, Gender, and Age, 1988 (Percent Using)

When Used, Gender, Age	Total	White Non-Latino	Black Non-Latino	Latino
Ever used				
Male				
12-17	45.3%	49.9%	29.7%	35.6%
18-25	77.7	79.7	69.3	74.2
Female				
12-17	39.2	43.2	25.1	36.2
18-25	72.4	78.0	56.5	54.7
Used on past month				
Male				
12-17	12.4	14.4	6.1	6.6
18-25	35.6	35.2	35.0	33.6
Female				
12-17	11.2	13.3	4.1	8.5
18-25	34.8	38.5	24.8	22.7

Note: These data are from the 1988 Household Survey on Drug Abuse. Excluded from the survey are persons in institutions (jails, prisons, juvenile detention facilities, long-term care health facilities), students in college dormitories, members of the military, and the homeless. Drug use among some of these groups is higher than it is among the general population. Hence the estimates of drug use in this table are conservative.

Source: U.S. Department of Health and Human Services, National Institute on Drug Abuse, *National Household Survey on Drug Abuse: Main Findings 1988* (1990), Tables 8.1, 8.3, and 8.5.

Table 3.8

Current Drug, Alcohol, and Cigarette Use Among Adolescents and Young Adults, by Specific Substance and Age, 1988 (Percent Using)

Age	Marijuana	Cocaine	Alcohol	Cigarettes
12-17	6.4%	1.1%	25.2%	11.8%
12-13	1.5	—	6.5	3.3
14-15	4.9	1.4	23.2	10.5
16-17	11.8	1.6	42.2	19.9
18-25	15.5	4.5	65.3	35.2
18-21	15.0	4.1	61.0	35.5
22-25	15.9	4.8	69.4	34.9

— Number too small to calculate a reliable rate.

Note: These data are from the 1988 Household Survey on Drug Abuse. Excluded from the survey are persons in institutions (jails, prisons, juvenile detention facilities, long-term care health facilities), students in college dormitories, members of the military, and the homeless. Drug use among some of these groups is higher than it is among the general population. Hence the estimates of drug use in this table are conservative.

Source: U.S. Department of Health and Human Services, National Institute on Drug Abuse, *National Household Survey on Drug Abuse: Main Findings 1988* (1990), Tables 3.4, 4.4, 7.4, and 8.4.

Table 3.9

Types of Substances Used by Adolescents and Young Adults, by Age and by Substance, 1988 (Percent Using)

When Used, Substance	Age 12-17	Age 18-25
Ever used		
Alcohol only	28.6%	32.3%
Illicit drugs only	3.1	0.9
Alcohol and drugs	21.6	58.0
1 substance only	31.3	32.9
2 different substances	12.8	29.6
3 or more different substances	9.2	28.7
Used in past month		
Alcohol only	18.5	48.7
Illicit drugs only	2.6	1.2
Alcohol and drugs	6.6	16.6
1 substance only	20.9	49.7
2 different substances	4.8	10.7
3 or more different substances	2.1	6.1

Note: These data are from the 1988 Household Survey on Drug Abuse. Excluded from the survey are persons in institutions (jails, prisons, juvenile detention facilities, long-term care health facilities), students in college dormitories, members of the military, and the homeless. Drug use among some of these groups is higher than it is among the general population. Hence the estimates of drug use in this table are conservative.

Source: U.S. Department of Health and Human Services, National Institute on Drug Abuse, *National Household Survey on Drug Abuse: Main Findings 1988* (1990), Tables 10.1 and 10.3.

Table 3.10

Average Age At First Use of Cigarettes, Alcohol, and Other Drugs, by Current Age, 1988

Substance	Age 12-17	Age 18-25
Cigarettes	11.6	13.5
Alcohol	13.1	15.4
Marijuana	13.4	15.4
Inhalants	12.5	14.7
Cocaine	14.9	18.0

Note: These data are from the 1988 Household Survey on Drug Abuse. Excluded from the survey are persons in institutions (jails, prisons, juvenile detention facilities, long-term care health facilities), students in college dormitories, members of the military, and the homeless. Drug use among some of these groups is higher than it is among the general population. Hence the estimates of drug use in this table are conservative.

Source: U.S. Department of Health and Human Services, National Institute on Drug Abuse, *National Household Survey on Drug Abuse: Main Findings 1988* (1990), Table 10.6.

Table 3.11

Drug and Alcohol Use by High School Seniors, by College Plans, 1990 (Percent Using)

When Used, Substance	College Plans: Complete Four Years	College Plans: None or Less Than Four Years
Ever used		
Marijuana	37.2%	48.0%
Inhalants	16.4	21.5
Hallucinogens	8.2	11.3
Cocaine	7.4	13.6
Crack	2.3	5.8
Heroin	1.0	1.9
Stimulants	14.5	24.2
Sedatives	4.6	5.6
Alcohol	89.4	90.4
Cigarettes	60.6	72.3
Used in past month		
Marijuana	11.9	17.6
Inhalants	2.4	3.3
Hallucinogens	2.0	2.3
Cocaine	1.4	2.6
Crack	0.4	1.3
Heroin	0.2	0.2
Stimulants	2.8	5.2
Sedatives	0.6	1.2
Alcohol	56.4	58.7
Cigarettes	25.4	37.5

Source: U.S. Department of Health and Human Services, press release on high school senior drug abuse survey, January 24, 1991, Tables 6 and 8.

Table 3.12

Trends in Daily Marijuana and Alcohol Use and in Binge Drinking Among High School Seniors, 1975-1990 (Percent)

Year	Daily Use in Past Month: Marijuana	Alcohol	Five or More Drinks in a Row in Past Two Weeks (Binge Drinking)
1975	6.0%	5.7%	36.8%
1976	8.2	5.6	37.1
1977	9.1	6.1	39.4
1978	10.7	5.7	40.3
1979	10.3	6.9	41.2
1980	9.1	6.0	41.2
1981	7.0	6.0	41.4
1982	6.3	5.7	40.5
1983	5.5	5.5	40.8
1984	5.0	4.8	38.7
1985	4.9	5.0	36.7
1986	4.0	4.8	36.8
1987	3.3	4.8	37.5
1988	2.7	4.2	34.7
1989	2.9	4.2	33.0
1990	2.2	3.7	32.2

Source: U.S. Department of Health and Human Services, press release on high school senior drug abuse survey, January 24, 1991, Table 13.

Fig. 3.3

Trends in Daily Marijuana and Alcohol Use Among High School Seniors, 1975-1990

Source: Table 3.12.

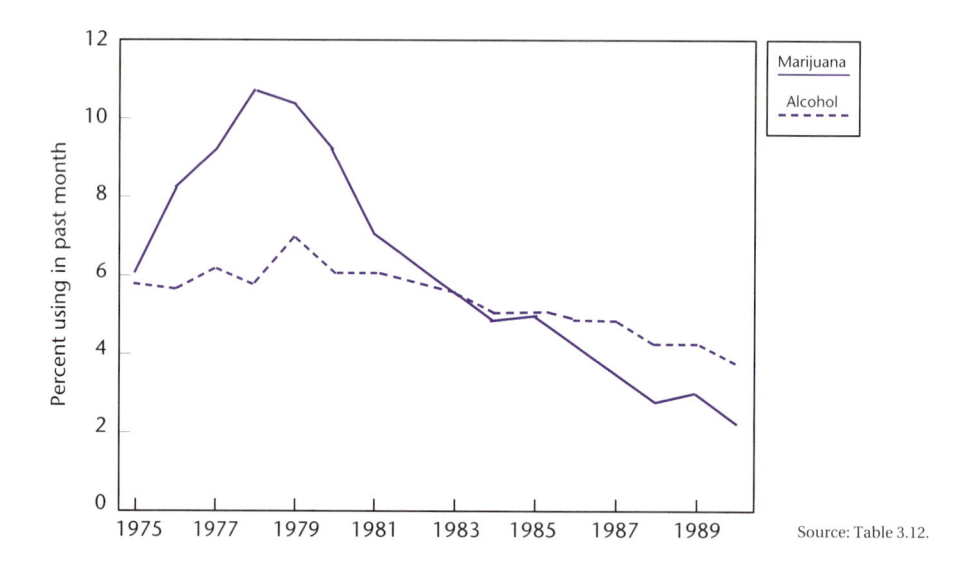

Fig. 3.4

Trends in Binge Drinking Among High School Seniors, 1975-1990

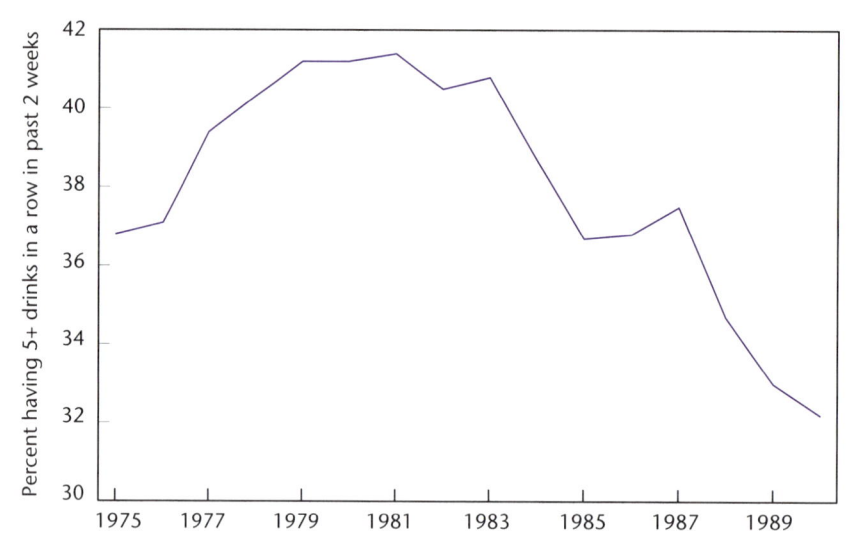

Source: Table 3.12.

Table 3.13

Trends in Arrest Rates Among 18-Year-Olds, by Gender and Type of Crime, 1965-1988 (Arrests Per 100,000 18-year-olds)

Gender, Year	Violent Crimes	Property Crimes	Weapons Violations	Drug Offenses
Both genders				
1965	338.4	1,849.6	123.3	102.1
1975	712.5	3,593.1	229.7	1,669.0
1985	660.9	3,399.2	268.3	1,239.1
1988	751.4	3,576.9	340.7	1,550.7
Male				
1965	637.5	3,290.7	234.7	178.6
1975	1,299.3	5,800.8	426.2	3,357.8
1985	1,193.8	5,429.0	501.2	2,167.8
1988	1,347.7	5,666.4	634.8	2,695.2
Female				
1965	37.4	399.4	11.2	25.2
1975	113.2	1,338.1	29.0	432.4
1985	114.3	1,333.0	28.3	282.6
1988	133.4	1,411.2	35.9	364.4

Source: U.S. Department of Justice, Federal Bureau of Investigation, *Age-Specific Arrest Rates and Race-Specific Arrest Rates for Selected Offenses: 1965-1988* (1990).

Table 3.14

Trends in Arrest Rates for Drunk Driving Among 18- to 24-Year-Olds, 1976-1986 (Arrests Per 100,000 Licensed Drivers in Age Group)

Age	1976	1981	1986
18	1,068	1,596	1,480
19	1,133	1,869	1,780
20	1,148	2,031	1,961
21	1,212	2,124	2,292
22	1,118	1,969	2,310
23	1,063	1,892	2,257
24	1,023	1,780	2,213
All ages	768	1,041	1,131

Source: U.S. Department of Justice, Bureau of Justice Statistics, *Drunk Driving* (1988), Table 2.

THE ADOLESCENT AND YOUNG ADULT FACT BOOK

Table 3.15

Committed Juvenile Offenders, by Race and Latino Origin and by Age, 1987

Age	Total	White	Black	Latino*
11-14	3,096	1,437	1,446	313
15-17	15,130	8,140	6,097	2,345
18 or older	6,798	3,712	2,753	2,087

*Persons of Latino origin can be of any race.

Note: Committed juvenile offenders are residents of long-term, state-operated juvenile facilities.

Source: U.S. Department of Justice, Bureau of Justice Statistics, *Correctional Populations in the United States, 1987* (1989), Table 4.1. Calculations by Children's Defense Fund.

Table 3.16

Primary Childhood Living Arrangements of Committed Juvenile Offenders, by Race and Latino Origin and by Age, 1987 (Percent)

Age, Living Arrangement	Total	White	Black	Latino*
Under 18				
Both parents	27.8%	32.7%	21.5%	29.4%
Mother only	50.2	47.9	53.7	51.0
Father only	5.9	8.0	3.6	4.3
Grandparents	10.3	6.0	15.7	9.8
Other relatives	2.4	1.5	3.3	1.9
Foster home	1.6	1.6	1.1	1.2
Other	1.8	2.3	1.1	2.4
18 or older				
Both parents	35.2	43.1	23.4	46.6
Mother only	43.7	38.5	52.9	35.3
Father only	4.9	5.1	3.4	3.8
Grandparents	9.1	5.8	13.9	7.7
Other relatives	3.9	3.9	3.5	4.4
Foster home	1.5	2.1	0.8	1.3
Other	1.7	1.5	2.1	0.9

*Persons of Latino origin can be of any race.

Note: Committed juvenile offenders are residents of long-term, state-operated juvenile facilities.

Source: U.S. Department of Justice, Bureau of Justice Statistics, *Correctional Populations in the United States, 1987* (1989), Table 4.3. Calculations by Children's Defense Fund.

Table 3.17

Alcohol and Drug Histories of Committed Juvenile Offenders, by Age, 1987 (Percent)

Substance, Use	Total	Under 18	18 or older
Alcohol			
Used regularly	57.1%	55.4%	61.7%
Under influence when committed current offense	31.9	31.9	31.7
Illegal drugs			
Used regularly	58.7	57.5	61.8
Under influence when committed current offense	39.4	39.1	40.3

Note: Committed juvenile offenders are residents of long-term, state-operated juvenile facilities.

Source: U.S. Department of Justice, Bureau of Justice Statistics, *Correctional Populations in the United States, 1987* (1989), Tables 4.19 and 4.23.

Table 3.18

Characteristics of Children in Custody, by Public or Private Status of the Facility, February 1, 1985 and February 15, 1989

Characteristic	1985 Public	1985 Private	1985 Total	1989 Public
Total children	49,322	34,080	83,402	56,123
Gender				
Male	42,549	23,844	66,393	49,443
Female	6,773	10,236	17,009	6,680
Race and Latino origin				
White	29,969	23,999	53,968	22,201
Black	18,269	9,204	27,473	33,922
Other*	1,084	877	1,961	1,415
Latino**	6,551	2,510	9,061	8,671
Age				
9 or younger	60	672	732	45
10-13	3,181	5,862	9,043	3,276
14-17	40,640	26,258	66,898	44,894
18 or older	5,441	1,288	6,729	7,908

*Includes American Indians, Alaskan Natives and Aleuts, Asians, and Pacific Islanders.
**Persons of Latino origin can be of any race.

Source: U.S. Department of Justice, Bureau of Justice Statistics, *Children in Custody, 1975-1985. Census of Public and Private Juvenile Detention, Correctional, and Shelter Facilities, 1975, 1977, 1979, 1983, and 1985* (1989), Table 31; and U.S. Department of Justice, Office of Juvenile Justice and Delinquency Prevention, *Public Juvenile Facilities: Children in Custody 1989* (1991), Table 2. Calculations by Children's Defense Fund.

Table 3.19

Juveniles Held in Public and Private Juvenile Facilities, by Gender and by Reason Held, February 1, 1985 (Percent of Total Held in Each Type of Facility)

Public–Private Control, Reason Held	Total	Male	Female
Public facilities			
Delinquent acts	93.4%	96.2%	76.1%
Violent offenses	24.8	26.4	15.2
Property offenses	44.6	47.0	30.1
Alcohol, drug offenses	5.4	5.5	5.0
Public order offenses, probation violation	13.2	12.1	19.7
All other offenses	5.4	5.3	6.0
Nondelinquent reasons	6.3	3.6	23.4
Status offenses*	4.6	2.6	17.7
Nonoffenders**	1.0	0.6	3.7
Voluntary admissions	0.6	0.4	2.1
Private facilities			
Delinquent acts	34.2	42.2	15.5
Violent offenses	5.4	6.9	2.0
Property offenses	17.3	22.0	6.2
Alcohol, drug offenses	2.0	2.4	1.1
Public order offenses, probation violation	1.9	2.1	1.6
All other offenses	7.5	8.8	4.5
Nondelinquent reasons	65.6	57.6	84.2
Status offenses*	19.7	16.8	26.7
Nonoffenders**	25.7	22.6	33.1
Voluntary admissions	20.1	18.2	24.5

*Status offenses are acts that are not criminal for adults, such as running away, truancy, and incorrigibility.

**Nonoffenders are those held for reasons not involving juvenile offenses, such as dependency, neglect, abuse, emotional disturbance, or mental retardation.

Note: The 1985 survey of children in custody was conducted on February 1, 1985. Because there is a great deal of movement in and out of these facilities, the figures above may not reflect the population of juveniles at other times. Facilities surveyed include juvenile detention, correctional, and shelter facilities.

Source: U.S. Department of Justice, Bureau of Justice Statistics, *Children in Custody, 1975-1985: Census of Public and Private Juvenile Detention, Correctional, and Shelter Facilities, 1975, 1977, 1979, 1983, and 1985* (1989), Table 41. Calculations by Children's Defense Fund.

Table 3.20

Criminal Victimization Among Adolescents and Young Adults, by Race, Type of Crime, Gender, and Age, 1988
(Rate Per 1,000 Population in Specified Group)

Type of Crime, Gender, Age	Total	White	Black
Crimes of violence*			
Male			
12-15	71.7	70.1	82.6
16-19	89.0	84.7	113.3
20-24	78.8	77.3	82.5
Female			
12-15	41.5	40.3	46.1
16-19	54.7	52.7	72.5
20-24	39.8	37.4	58.7
Crimes of theft**			
Male			
12-15	102.2	96.4	120.2
16-19	123.2	129.2	92.6
20-24	136.2	142.0	92.0
Female			
12-15	122.8	127.3	114.2
16-19	118.6	126.8	79.5
20-24	111.0	112.8	104.8

*Crimes of violence include rape, robbery, and assault; murder and manslaughter are excluded.

**Crimes of theft include theft of property or cash by stealth, with or without personal contact; if there is personal contact, there is no force or threat of force.

Source: U.S. Department of Justice, Bureau of Justice Statistics, *Criminal Victimization in the United States, 1988* (1990), Tables 5 and 10.

Fig. 3.5

Criminal Victimization Among Adolescents and Young Adults, by Race, Gender, and Age, Violent Crimes, 1988

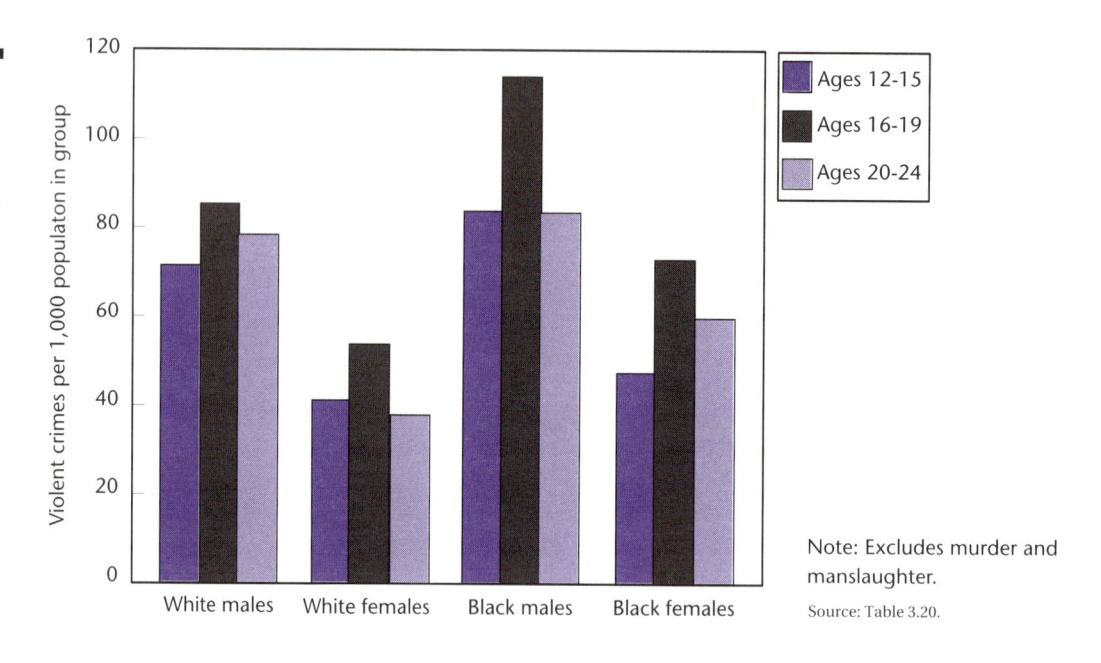

Note: Excludes murder and manslaughter.
Source: Table 3.20.

Table 3.21

Average Annual Rate of Handgun Crime* Victimization, by Race, Gender, and Age, 1979-1987 (Rate Per 1,000 Population in Specified Group)

Gender, Age	White	Black
Male		
12-15	1.5	6.4
16-19	7.2	24.0
20-24	9.7	22.0
Female		
12-15	1.0	2.7
16-19	3.4	8.1
20-24	3.4	8.6

*Excludes murder and manslaughter committed with handguns.

Source: U.S. Department of Justice, Bureau of Justice Statistics, *Handgun Crime Victims* (1990), Table 4.

Fig. 3.6

Handgun Crime Victimization Among Adolescents and Young Adults, by Race, Gender, and Age, Annual Average, 1979-1987

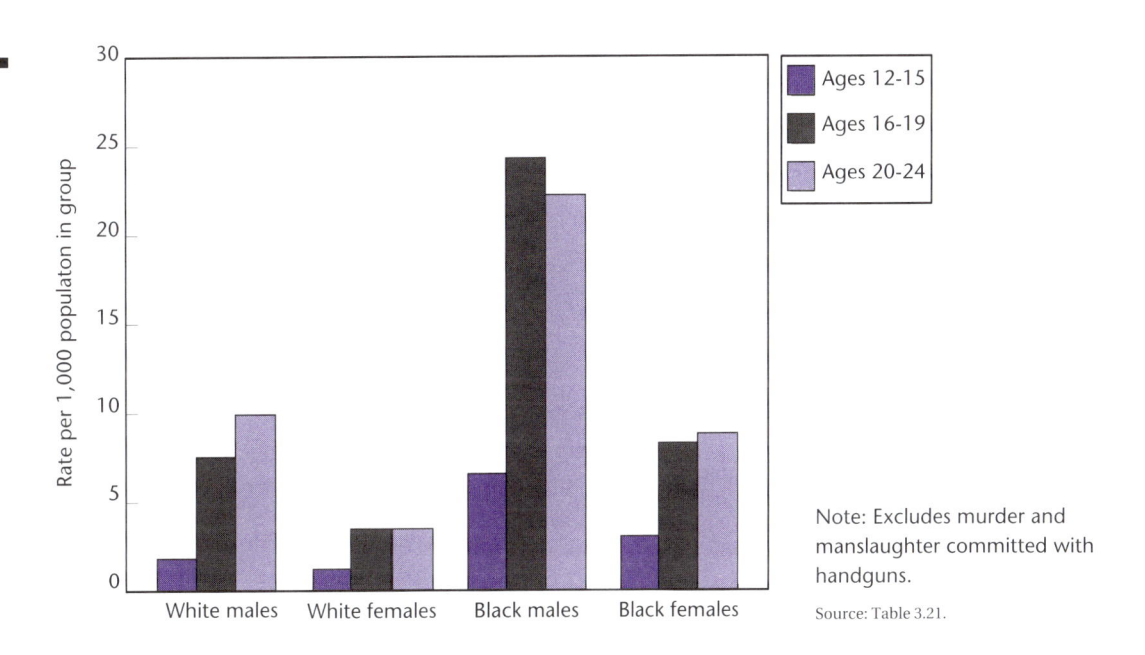

Note: Excludes murder and manslaughter committed with handguns.

Source: Table 3.21.

EDUCATION

More than ever before, educational achievement is the key to national prosperity and adult opportunity. Yet there is abundant evidence that our public schools are not preparing American students—especially poor and minority students—to meet the challenges ahead. Although graduation rates generally have improved in recent decades, about 20 percent of all American students still do not graduate from high school, and in some cities the proportion is much higher. But even among those who graduate, many are poorly equipped to maintain America's competitiveness in the international economy. International achievement tests show, for example, that American students rank at or near the bottom in math and science. In addition, too few of our graduates have the skills and the habits that foster lifelong learning, citizen participation, and personal fulfillment.

Enrollment

School enrollment among youths age 16 and older has increased since 1960. By 1988 more than half of all teens were enrolled, including most 16- and 17-year-olds. One-quarter of 18- and 19-year-olds enrolled in school still are attending high school, however. Although almost the same proportion of male and female teenagers is enrolled in school, older male teens are about twice as likely as their female peers to be attending high school rather than college.

Among teenagers younger than 16, there are no racial or ethnic differences in enrollment. Among those 16 and older, however, Latinos are less likely than either blacks or whites to be enrolled in school. Racial and ethnic differences in enrollment among older teens are more pronounced among males than females. Further, older black and Latino teenage males are more likely than their white counterparts to be completing high school instead of enrolling in college. Latino teens and young adults are more likely than either blacks or whites to be enrolled below the college level.

Blacks and Latinos are more likely than whites to be two or more grades behind in school, and males are more likely than females to be behind. Among males ages 16 and 17, approximately one in seven blacks and one in eight Latinos is two or more years behind in school, compared with only one in 16 whites. Among females, approximately one in 10 blacks, one in seven Latinas, and one in 26 whites is two or more grades behind.

It is not that black or Latino youths are somehow less capable academically. They have not failed in school. Rather, school has failed them. School segregation, differences in school quality, tracking, poverty, and other systematic biases all have been shown to contribute to minority students' lower overall educational achievement.

The school experience

School segregation is still a major factor for blacks and Latinos. In 1986 almost one-third of all black and Latino students attended schools in which 90 percent or more of the students were from minority groups; approximately two-thirds attended schools in which more than half the students were from minority groups. During the past two decades, the proportion of Latino children in predominantly minority schools has increased, while the proportion of black children in such schools has decreased somewhat.

Within schools, there are marked differences among racial and ethnic groups in the quality of the school experience. Black and Latino students are less likely than white and Asian students to be enrolled in academic (college preparatory) programs, and more likely to be enrolled in remedial and special education courses.

Blacks are at least twice as likely to be enrolled in programs for the educable mentally retarded as are children in other racial or ethnic groups. Asian children are the least likely of any racial group to be in any special education program for students with disabilities.

Asian students are several times more likely than students from any other racial or ethnic group to take advanced math and science courses in high school. Almost one-fourth of all Asian students take AP (advanced placement) calculus, compared with less than 3 percent of all other students. Asian students are at least three times as likely to take AP chemistry or physics than students from any other racial or ethnic group.

Blacks are about twice as likely as Latinos, whites, or Native Americans to be suspended from school or to be corporally punished. Asian Americans are only half as likely as Latinos, whites, or Native Americans to be suspended, and even less likely to be corporally punished.

Achievement

Almost all 17-year-olds reach the "basic" level of proficiency in reading, math, and science, but only 40 to 50 percent of them become "adept" in these areas, as defined by the National Assessment of Educational Progress. At all ages, females generally outperform males in reading; by age 13, males have an advantage in science, and by age 17 they have an advantage in both math and science.

Black and Latino 17-year-olds have about the same proficiency scores as white students at age 13. White 17-year-olds are about twice as likely to be adept in reading, math, and science as are their black and Latino peers. In general, student proficiency levels increase as parents' education levels increase.

Asians score higher on the math portion of the SAT college admission exam than any other racial or ethnic group. Whites score highest on the verbal subtest.

Attainment

An increasing percentage of young adults are high school graduates. There are only small differences in the graduation rates of blacks and whites, and both groups are much more likely than Latinos to graduate. Blacks, however, take longer than whites to complete high school. Almost one-fifth of young Latino adults have no high school education at all, and two-fifths are not graduates. Since 1970 there has been either no improvement or a worsening in the Latino dropout rate, depending on the age group.

Whites are more likely to be in college or to have attended college than are either blacks or Latinos. Nearly half of white 20- to 24-year-olds complete some college, compared with one-third of their black and one-fourth of their Latino age peers. Approximately one in 12 white high school graduates obtains a bachelor's degree within four years of completing high school, but only one in 30 black and one in 50 Latino graduates completes college within four years of high school graduation.

Poverty is strongly associated with low educational attainment. Among 20- and 21-year-olds, poor youths are less likely than their nonpoor peers to be enrolled in school or to be high school graduates. Longitudinal research has found that poverty during the teen years is associated with a lower probability of graduating from high school. Racial differences in both school enrollment and graduation rates are small when income levels are held constant.

In the past decade or so, income has become an increasingly important factor in college-going. In 1975 there was very little difference in college attendance between poor and nonpoor high school graduates, and only a small difference between blacks and whites. By 1987, however, poor graduates were much less likely than their nonpoor counterparts to have attended college. The increased black–white gap in college attendance is accounted for primarily by the decreased college attendance rate among poor high school graduates. It's not surprising, therefore, that youths from high socioeconomic status (SES) families—mostly white youths—are more likely than those from low SES families to earn a bachelor's degree within four years of high school graduation.

Table 4.1

Trends in School Enrollment, by Age, Level, and Gender, 1960-1988 (Percent)

Level, Gender, Year	14-15	16-17	Age 18-19	20-21	22-24
Percent of population enrolled					
Total, both genders					
1960	97.8%	82.6%	38.4%	19.4%	8.7%
1970	98.1	90.0	47.7	31.9	14.9
1980	98.2	89.0	46.4	31.0	16.3
1988	98.9	91.6	55.7	39.1	18.3
Male					
1960	97.9	84.5	47.8	27.1	15.0
1970	98.2	91.3	54.4	42.7	21.2
1980	98.7	89.1	47.0	32.6	17.8
1988	98.9	92.1	56.2	39.0	20.5
Female					
1960	97.6	80.6	30.0	13.1	3.4
1970	98.0	88.6	41.6	23.6	9.4
1980	97.7	88.8	45.8	29.5	14.9
1988	98.8	91.2	55.2	39.1	16.2
Percent of those enrolled who are below college level					
Total, both genders					
1960	100.0	95.2	28.5	3.3	4.5
1970	100.0	96.2	21.9	4.7	4.0
1980	99.9	96.6	22.6	3.7	3.2
1988	100.0	97.2	25.0	1.5	1.3
Male					
1960	100.0	95.8	31.0	2.7	1.9
1970	100.0	96.3	26.1	4.2	3.1
1980	99.9	97.4	27.1	2.7	3.0
1988	100.0	98.3	32.8	2.3	1.1
Female					
1960	100.0	94.5	25.1	4.3	14.0
1970	100.0	96.2	16.9	5.4	5.6
1980	99.9	95.8	18.1	4.6	3.3
1988	100.0	96.1	17.1	0.9	1.7

Sources: U.S. Department of Commerce, Bureau of the Census, *Current Population Reports*, Series P-20, No. 110, School Enrollment, and Education of Young Adults and Their Fathers: October 1960 (1961), Tables 2 and 5; U.S. Department of Commerce, Bureau of the Census, *Current Population Reports*, Series P-20, No. 222, School Enrollment: October 1970 (1971), Table 1; U.S. Department of Commerce, Bureau of the Census, *Current Population Reports*, Series P-20, No. 400, School Enrollment—Social and Economic Characteristics of Students: October 1981 and October 1980 (1985), Table 26; and U.S. Department of Commerce, Bureau of the Census, *Current Population Reports*, Series P-20, No. 443, School Enrollment—Social and Economic Characteristics of Students: October 1988 and 1987 (1990), Table 1. Calculations by Children's Defense Fund.

Table 4.2

School Enrollment, by Race and Latino Origin, Level, Gender, and Age, 1988 (Percent)

Level, Gender, Age	Total	White	Black	Latino*
Percent of population enrolled				
Total, both genders				
14-15	98.9%	98.8%	98.9%	98.8%
16-17	91.6	91.4	91.5	78.8
18-19	55.7	55.8	50.3	44.1
20-21	39.1	40.2	28.1	16.7
22-24	18.3	18.6	13.2	12.1
Male				
14-15	98.9	98.9	99.1	98.1
16-17	92.1	91.6	93.2	80.9
18-19	56.2	56.5	49.7	44.7
20-21	39.0	40.9	20.7	21.6
22-24	20.5	20.7	14.7	12.5
Female				
14-15	98.8	98.8	98.6	99.6
16-17	91.2	91.1	89.8	76.6
18-19	55.2	55.1	50.9	43.5
20-21	39.1	39.6	34.3	11.2
22-24	16.2	16.5	11.9	11.5
Percent of those enrolled who are below college level				
Total, both genders				
14-15	100.0	100.0	100.0	100.0
16-17	97.2	97.4	96.8	97.6
18-19	25.0	20.9	47.2	37.0
20-21	1.5	1.7	1.1	12.0
22-24	1.3	1.1	1.5	2.1
Male				
14-15	100.0	100.0	100.0	100.0
16-17	98.3	98.2	98.9	96.5
18-19	32.8	29.0	57.5	54.0
20-21	2.3	2.4	3.2	11.6
22-24	1.1	0.5	2.9	0.0
Female				
14-15	100.0	100.0	100.0	100.0
16-17	96.1	96.6	94.6	98.3
18-19	17.1	12.8	37.8	19.9
20-21	0.9	1.0	0.0	10.3
22-24	1.7	2.0	0.0	4.8

*Persons of Latino origin can be of any race.

Source: U.S. Department of Commerce, Bureau of the Census, *Current Population Reports*, Series P-20, No. 443, School Enrollment—Social and Economic Characteristics of Students: October 1988 and 1987 (1990), Table 1. Calculations by Children's Defense Fund.

Table 4.3

Trends in School Enrollment, by Race and Latino Origin, Level, and Age, 1970-1988 (Percent)

Level, Gender, Age	Total	White	Black	Latino*
Percent of population enrolled				
1970				
14-15	98.1%	98.2%	97.6%	NA
16-17	90.0	90.6	85.7	NA
18-19	47.7	48.7	40.1	NA
20-21	31.9	33.1	22.8	NA
22-24	14.9	15.7	8.0	NA
1980				
14-15	98.2	98.3	97.9	94.3%
16-17	89.0	88.6	90.6	81.8
18-19	46.4	46.3	45.7	37.8
20-21	31.0	31.9	23.4	19.5
22-24	16.3	16.4	13.6	11.7
1988				
14-15	98.9	98.8	98.9	98.8
16-17	91.6	91.4	91.5	78.8
18-19	55.7	55.8	50.3	44.1
20-21	39.1	40.2	28.1	16.7
22-24	18.3	18.6	13.2	12.1
Percent of those enrolled who are below college level				
1970				
14-15	100.0	100.0	100.0	NA
16-17	96.2	96.2	97.5	NA
18-19	21.9	19.3	45.7	NA
20-21	4.7	3.8	12.6	NA
22-24	4.0	3.5	11.9	NA
1980				
14-15	99.9	99.9	100.0	100.0
16-17	96.6	96.5	97.1	98.0
18-19	22.6	19.4	42.7	39.4
20-21	3.7	3.4	7.0	15.3
22-24	3.2	2.6	8.2	9.7
1988				
14-15	100.0	100.0	100.0	100.0
16-17	97.2	97.4	96.8	97.6
18-19	25.0	20.9	47.2	37.0
20-21	1.5	1.7	1.1	12.0
22-24	1.3	1.1	1.5	2.1

*Persons of Latino origin can be of any race.
NA— Data not available.

Sources: U.S. Department of Commerce, Bureau of the Census, *Current Population Reports*, Series P-20, No. 222, School Enrollment: October 1970 (1971), Table 1; U.S. Department of Commerce, Bureau of the Census, *Current Population Reports*, Series P-20, No. 400, School Enrollment—Social and Economic Characteristics of Students: October 1981 and October 1980 (1985), Table 26; and U.S. Department of Commerce, Bureau of the Census, *Current Population Reports*, Series P-20, No. 443, School Enrollment—Social and Economic Characteristics of Students: October 1988 and 1987 (1990), Table 1. Calculations by Children's Defense Fund.

Table 4.4

Students Behind in School, by Gender, Age, and Race and Latino Origin, 1988 (Percent Enrolled Two or More Years Behind Modal Grade)

Gender, Age	Total	White	Black	Latino*
Male				
10-13	5.2%	4.1%	10.3%	6.1%
14-15	7.9	6.4	17.9	13.1
16-17	7.7	6.0	15.1	13.8
18-19	10.6	4.2	23.2	22.7
Female				
10-13	3.3	2.9	5.4	6.7
14-15	3.5	2.8	6.7	3.6
16-17	4.8	3.8	9.8	15.0
18-19	6.2	3.7	21.1	9.3

*Persons of Latino origin can be of any race.

Source: U.S. Department of Commerce, Bureau of the Census, *Current Population Reports*, Series P-20, No. 443, School Enrollment—Social and Economic Characteristics of Students: October 1988 and 1987 (1990), Table 3. Calculations by Children's Defense Fund.

Fig. 4.1

Adolescents Behind In School, by Race and Latino Origin, Age, and Gender, 1988

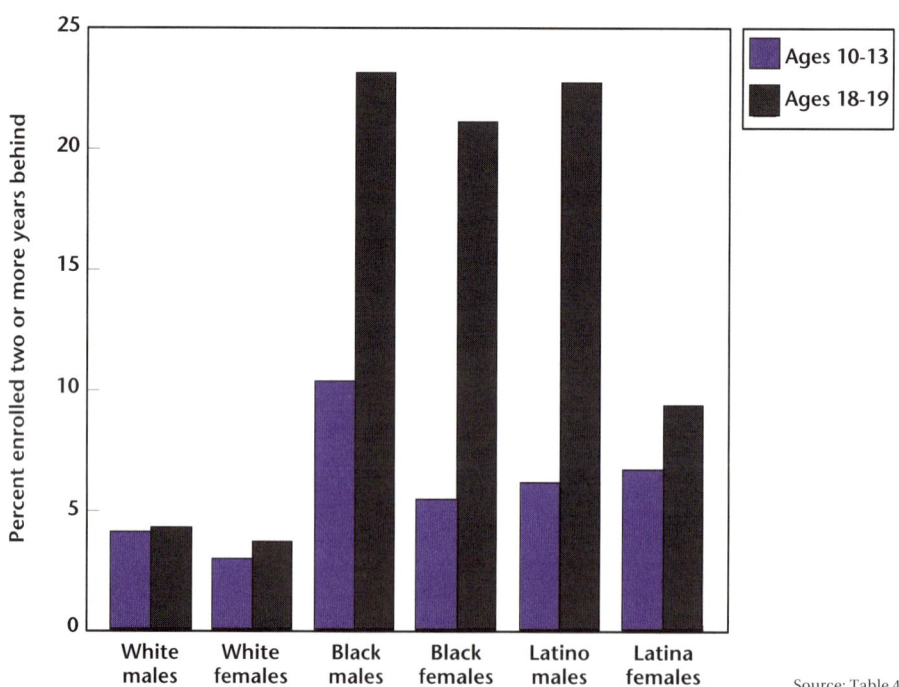

Source: Table 4.4.

CHILDREN'S DEFENSE FUND

Table 4.5

Special Education Placements, by Race and Latino Origin, 1986 (Percent in Special Education Programs)

Programs For:	Total	Native American	Latino	Non-Latino White	Non-Latino Black	Asian
Educable mentally retarded	1.1%	1.1%	0.6%	0.9%	2.3%	0.2%
Speech impaired	2.5	2.8	2.0	2.6	2.5	1.6
Emotionally impaired	0.6	0.5	0.5	0.6	1.0	0.1
Learning disabled	4.3	5.7	4.3	4.3	4.4	1.6

Source: U.S. Department of Education, Office for Civil Rights, *1986 Elementary and Secondary School Civil Rights Survey: National Summaries* (1987), Table 1. Calculations by Children's Defense Fund.

Table 4.6

Trends in School Desegregation for Black and Latino Children, 1968-1986 (Percent in Segregated Schools)

Degree of Segregation, Year	Black	Latino*
Predominantly minority (more than 50% minority)		
1968	76.6%	54.8%
1972	63.6	56.6
1980	63.5	70.6
1984	63.5	70.6
1986	63.3	71.5
Intensely minority (more than 90% minority)		
1968	64.3	23.1
1972	38.7	23.3
1980	33.2	28.8
1984	33.2	31.0
1986	32.5	32.2

Source: Gary Orfield, Franklin Monfort, and Melissa Aaron, *Status of School Desegregation, 1968-1986*, A Report of the Council of Urban Boards of Education and the National School Desegregation Research Project, University of Chicago (1989), Table 1.

Fig. 4.2

School Desegregation for Black and Latino Children, 1968 and 1986

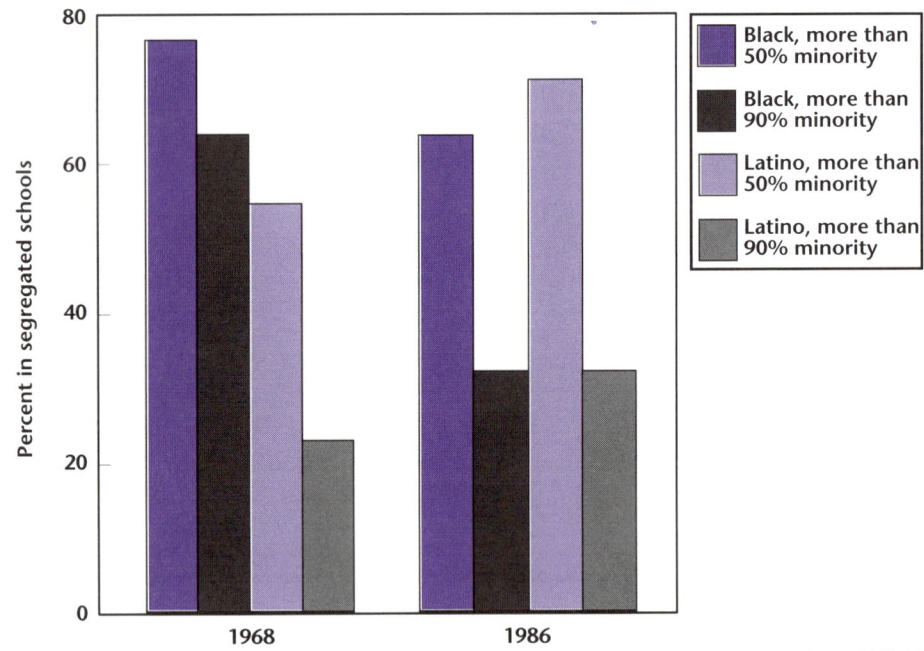

Legend:
- Black, more than 50% minority
- Black, more than 90% minority
- Latino, more than 50% minority
- Latino, more than 90% minority

Source: Table 4.6.

Table 4.7

Math and Science Course-Taking Patterns, by Race and Latino Origin, 1987 High School Graduates (Percent Taking Each Course)

Course	White	Black	Latino	Asian	Other*
Mathematics					
Algebra I	77.7%	70.7%	73.1%	68.5%	78.0%
Algebra II	51.9	32.4	30.2	67.1	28.4
Geometry	65.1	44.0	40.2	81.4	48.4
Trigonometry	20.9	10.9	9.9	42.1	6.5
Analysis/ pre-calculus	13.5	5.1	7.4	39.6	7.5
Calculus	5.9	2.3	3.6	29.8	3.2
AP calculus	2.8	1.4	2.6	23.9	1.3
Remedial/below grade course	20.6	46.5	42.5	16.3	40.7
Science					
Biology	89.2	86.2	85.4	91.5	88.8
AP/honors biology	2.8	1.5	1.6	4.3	0.9
Chemistry	47.7	29.8	29.4	69.9	30.1
AP/honors chemistry	3.5	1.2	2.3	13.9	0.8
Physics	20.9	10.1	9.8	47.1	11.5
AP/honors physics	1.7	0.4	0.8	5.7	1.8

*Includes American Indians, Alaskan Natives, and Aleuts.

Source: Andrew Kolstad and Judy Thorne, *Changes in High School Course Work From 1982 to 1987: Evidence from Two National Surveys*, Paper presented at the Annual Meeting of the American Educational Research Association, March 27, 1989, based on unpublished tabulations from the U.S. Department of Education, National Center for Education Statistics, Tables 7 and 8.

Fig. 4.3

High School Graduates Who Took Selected Math Courses, by Race and Latino Origin, 1987

*Includes American Indians, Alaskan Natives, and Aleuts.

Source: Table 4.7.

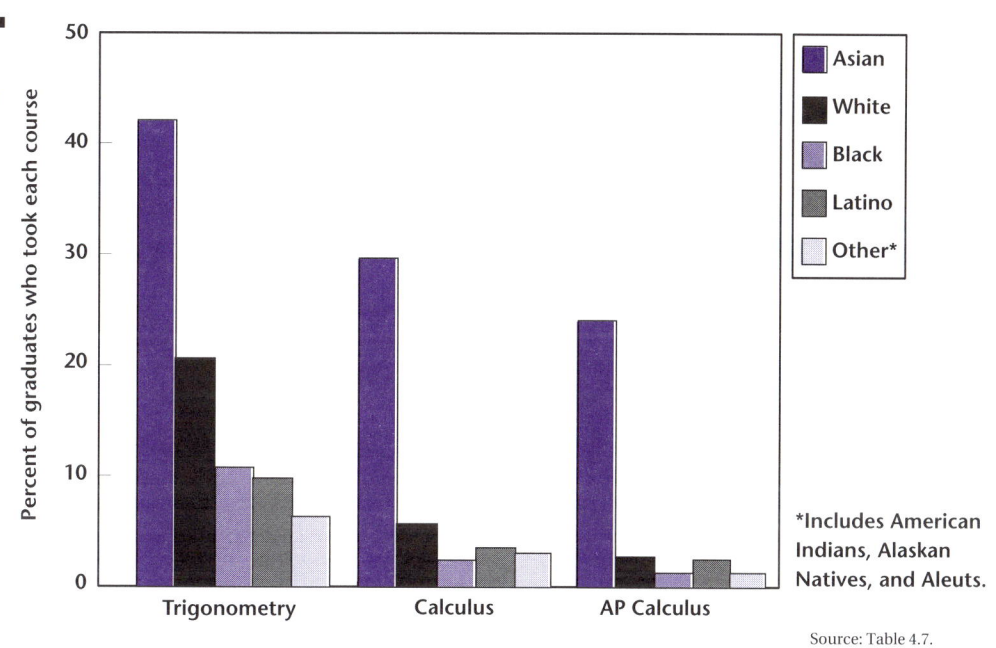

Table 4.8

Suspension and Corporal Punishment, by Race and Latino Origin, 1986 (Percent)

	Total	Native American	Latino	Non-Latino White	Non-Latino Black	Asian
Suspension	4.8%	4.1%	4.4%	4.0%	9.1%	2.3%
Corporal punishment	2.7	2.5	2.0	2.3	5.2	0.3

Source: U.S. Department of Education, Office for Civil Rights, *1986 Elementary and Secondary School Civil Rights Survey: National Summaries* (1987), Table 1. Calculations by Children's Defense Fund.

THE ADOLESCENT AND YOUNG ADULT FACT BOOK

Table 4.9

Students At or Above Different Proficiency Levels, by Subject and Age, 1986 and 1988 (Percent)

Subject, Age	Basic	Intermediate	Adept
Reading			
9	62.5%	17.0%	1.2%
13	95.1	58.0	10.6
17	98.9	86.2	41.8
Math			
9	73.9	20.8	0.6
13	98.5	73.1	15.9
17	99.9	96.0	51.1
Science			
9	71.4	27.6	3.4
13	91.8	53.4	9.4
17	96.7	80.8	41.4

Note: Reading data are for 1988, math and science data are for 1986.

Sources: U.S. Department of Education, Office of Educational Research and Improvement, *The Reading Report Card, 1971-88, Trends From the Nation's Report Card* (1990), pp. 55-56, 59-60, and 63-64; Educational Testing Service, *The Mathematics Report Card: Are We Measuring Up? Trends and Achievement Based on the 1986 National Assessment* (1988), pp. 139-141; and Educational Testing Service, *The Science Report Card: Elements of Risk and Recovery, Trends and Achievement Based on the 1986 National Assessment* (1988), pp. 147-149.

Table 4.10

Students At or Above Expected Level of Proficiency, by Gender, Age, and Subject, 1986 and 1988 (Percent At or Above Expected Level of Proficiency)

Age, Expected Proficiency, Subject	Male	Female	Difference*
9 (Basic)			
Reading	58.1%	66.9%	8.8
Math	74.0	73.9	-0.1
Science	72.7	70.1	-2.6
13 (Intermediate)			
Reading	51.3	64.6	13.3
Math	74.0	72.3	-1.7
Science	58.4	48.4	-10.0
17 (Adept)			
Reading	37.3	45.9	8.6
Math	54.2	48.1	-6.1
Science	49.3	33.8	-15.5

*Difference = female - male; difference is in percentage points.

Note: Reading data are for 1988, math and science data are for 1986.

Sources: U.S. Department of Education, Office of Educational Research and Improvement, *The Reading Report Card, 1971-88, Trends From the Nation's Report Card* (1990), pp. 55, 59, and 63; Educational Testing Service, *The Mathematics Report Card: Are We Measuring Up? Trends and Achievement Based on the 1986 National Assessment* (1988), pp. 139-141; and Educational Testing Service, *The Science Report Card: Elements of Risk and Recovery, Trends and Achievement Based on the 1986 National Assessment* (1988), pp. 147-149.

Table 4.11

Average Achievement Scores, by Race and Latino Origin, Subject, and Age, 1986-1988

Subject, Age	Total	White	Black	Latino*
Reading				
9	211.8	217.7	188.5	193.7
13	257.5	261.3	242.9	240.1
17	290.1	294.7	274.4	270.8
Math				
9	221.7	226.9	201.6	205.4
13	269.0	273.6	249.2	254.3
17	302.0	307.5	278.6	283.1
Science				
9	224.3	231.9	199.4	196.2
13	251.4	259.2	221.6	226.1
17	288.5	297.5	259.3	252.8

*Persons of Latino origin can be of any race.

Note: Reading data are for 1988, math and science data are for 1986.

Sources: U.S. Department of Education, Office of Educational Research and Improvement, *The Reading Report Card, 1971-88, Trends From the Nation's Report Card* (1990), pp. 54, 58, and 62; Educational Testing Service, *The Mathematics Report Card: Are We Measuring Up? Trends and Achievement Based on the 1986 National Assessment* (1988), p. 138; and Educational Testing Service, *The Science Report Card: Elements of Risk and Recovery, Trends and Achievement Based on the 1986 National Assessment* (1988), p. 146.

Table 4.12

Student Achievement At or Above Expected Level of Proficiency, by Age, and Race and Latino Origin (Percent At or Above Expected Level of Proficiency)

Age, Expected Proficiency, Subject	Total	White	Black	Latino*
Age 9 (Basic)				
Reading	62.5%	68.3%	39.2%	46.9%
Math	73.9	79.2	53.3	58.7
Science	71.4	78.4	49.1	45.1
Age 13 (Intermediate)				
Reading	58.0	63.3	39.2	34.9
Math	73.1	78.7	49.4	55.2
Science	53.4	61.9	27.6	20.2
Age 17 (Adept)				
Reading	41.8	46.3	25.8	24.3
Math	51.1	58.0	21.7	26.8
Science	41.4	48.8	15.5	12.3

*Persons of Latino origin can be of any race.

Note: Reading data are for 1988, math and science data are for 1986.

Sources: U.S. Department of Education, Office of Educational Research and Improvement, *The Reading Report Card, 1971-88, Trends From the Nation's Report Card* (1990), pp. 55, 59, and 63; Educational Testing Service, *The Mathematics Report Card: Are We Measuring Up? Trends and Achievement Based on the 1986 National Assessment* (1988), pp. 139-141; and Educational Testing Service, *The Science Report Card: Elements of Risk and Recovery, Trends and Achievement Based on the 1986 National Assessment* (1988), pp. 147-149.

Fig. 4.4

Students Reading At or Above Expected Level of Proficiency, by Race and Latino Origin and by Age, 1988

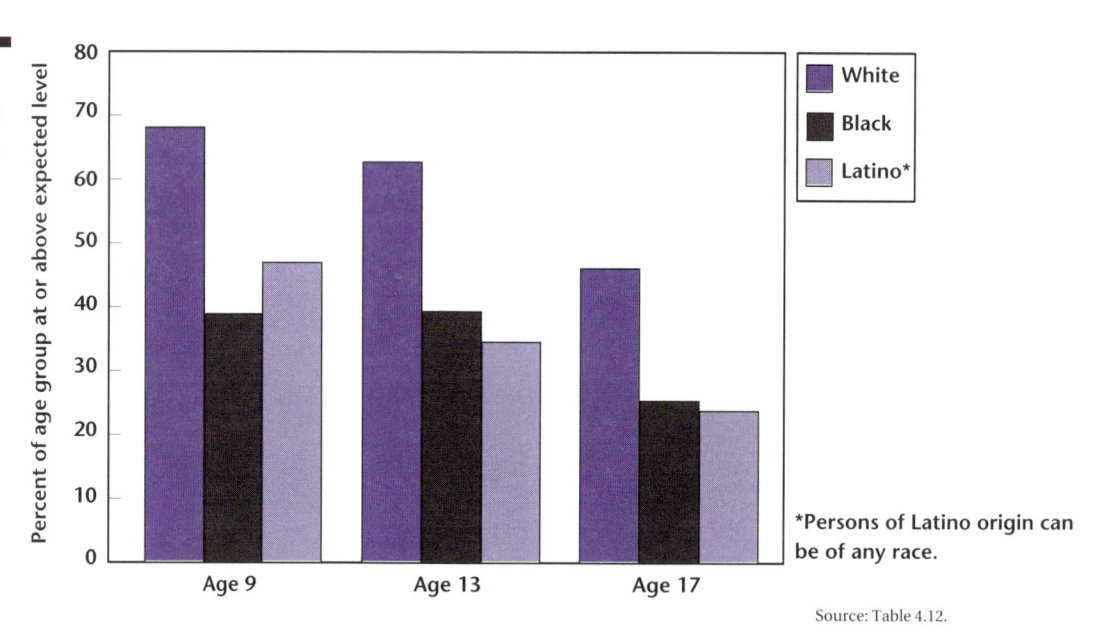

*Persons of Latino origin can be of any race.

Source: Table 4.12.

Table 4.13

Student Reading and Math Achievement, by Age and Parents' Education, 1986 and 1988 (Percent At or Above Specified Level of Proficiency)

Age, Subject, Parents' Education	Basic	Intermediate	Adept
Age 9			
Reading			
Less than high school	47.7%	6.4%	0.0%
High school graduate	59.9	16.7	0.5
Post high school	70.3	22.6	2.0
Math			
Less than high school	49.4	6.2	0.0
High school graduate	72.5	17.4	0.1
Some post high school	79.7	26.4	0.8
College graduate	82.5	29.4	1.1
Age 13			
Reading			
Less than high school	92.1	43.8	5.9
High school graduate	95.2	54.3	6.0
Post high school	96.8	66.4	15.4
Math			
Less than high school	96.9	56.3	5.3
High school graduate	98.5	68.9	7.8
Some post high school	99.5	80.3	17.7
College graduate	99.1	83.0	25.6
Age 17			
Reading			
Less than high school	98.3	70.2	14.5
High school graduate	98.8	82.3	31.9
Post high school	99.5	92.4	52.1
Math			
Less than high school	100.0	90.2	20.0
High school graduate	100.0	94.3	39.3
Some post high school	100.0	97.7	54.1
College graduate	100.0	98.4	68.0

Note: Reading data are for 1988, math and science data are for 1986.

Sources: U.S. Department of Education, Office of Educational Research and Improvement, *The Reading Report Card, 1971-88, Trends From the Nation's Report Card* (1990), pp. 55-56, 59-60, and 63-64; and Educational Testing Service, *The Mathematics Report Card: Are We Measuring Up? Trends and Achievement Based on the 1986 National Assessment* (1988), pp. 139-141.

Table 4.14

Average SAT Scores, by Racial and Ethnic Group, 1990

Racial/Ethnic Group	Verbal	Math
American Indian/Alaskan Native	388	437
Asian American/Pacific Islander	410	528
Black	352	385
Latino		
Mexican American	380	429
Puerto Rican	359	405
Other	383	434
White	442	491
Other	410	467

Source: The College Board, *College Bound Seniors, 1990 Profile of SAT and Achievement Test Takers* (1990), p. 6.

Table 4.15

Trends in Enrollment and Educational Attainment of 18- to 24-Year-Olds, by Race and Latino Origin, 1967-1988 (Percent)

Category, Year	Total	White	Black	Latino*
Percent of population who are high school graduates				
1967	75.5%	78.0%	55.9%	NA
1970	78.8	81.4	59.5	NA
1975	80.8	83.2	64.8	57.5%
1980	80.9	82.6	69.7	54.1
1985	82.4	83.6	75.6	62.9
1988	81.2	82.3	75.1	55.2
Percent of population who are enrolled in college				
1967	25.5	26.9	13.0	NA
1970	25.7	27.1	15.5	NA
1975	26.3	26.9	20.7	20.4
1980	25.6	26.2	19.2	16.1
1985	27.8	28.7	19.8	16.9
1988	30.3	31.3	21.1	17.0
Percent of high school graduates who are enrolled in college				
1967	33.7	34.5	23.3	NA
1970	32.7	33.2	26.0	NA
1975	32.5	32.4	32.0	35.5
1980	31.6	31.8	27.6	29.8
1985	33.7	34.4	26.1	26.9
1988	37.3	38.1	28.1	30.9

*Persons of Latino origin can be of any race.
NA — Data not available.

Source: U.S. Department of Commerce, Bureau of the Census, *Current Population Reports*, Series P-20, No. 443, School Enrollment—Social and Economic Characteristics of Students: October 1988 and 1987 (1990), Table A-7. Calculations by Children's Defense Fund.

Table 4.16

Years of School Completed Among 20- to 24-Year-Olds, by Race and Latino Origin, 1988 (Percent)

Years of School Completed	Total	White	Black	Latino*
8 or fewer	3.9%	4.0%	3.4%	18.0%
9 to 11	11.4	10.4	17.8	21.8
12 (high school graduate)	41.8	41.4	46.5	35.8
13+ (some college)	41.5	44.1	32.3	24.4

*Persons of Latino origin can be of any race.

Source: U.S. Department of Commerce, Bureau of the Census, *Current Population Reports*, Series P-20, No. 428, Educational Attainment in the United States: March 1987 and 1986 (1988), Table 1. Calculations by Children's Defense Fund.

Fig. 4.5

Years of School Completed by 20- to 24-Year-Olds, by Race and Latino Origin, 1988

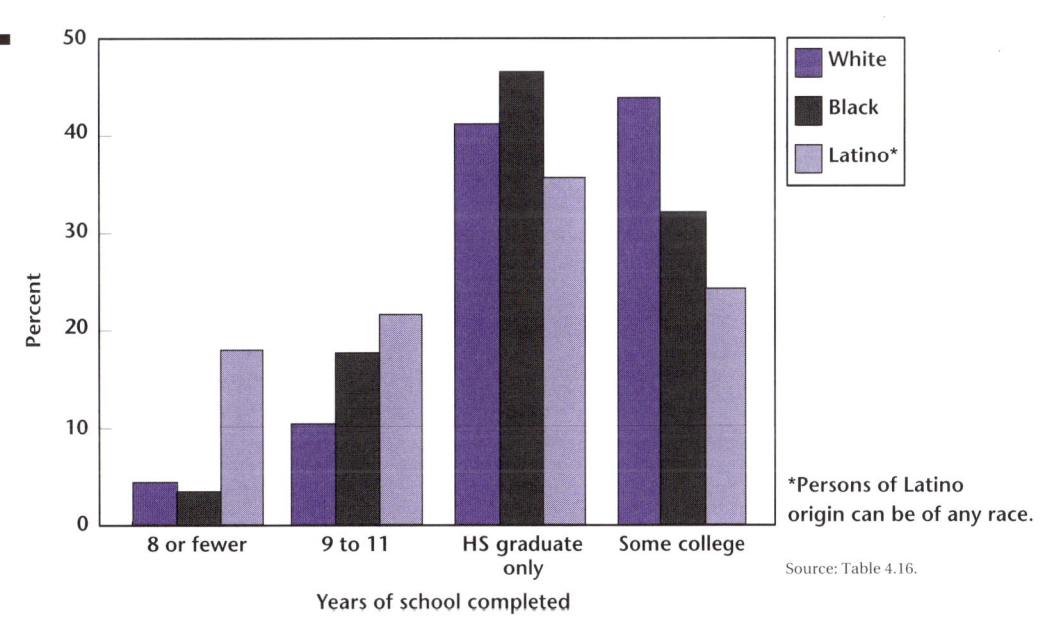

*Persons of Latino origin can be of any race.

Source: Table 4.16.

Table 4.17

Trends in Dropout Rates, by Race and Latino Origin, and by Age, 1970-1988 (Percent Not Enrolled, Not High School Graduate)

Age, Year	Total	White	Black	Latino*
16-17				
1970	8.0%	7.3%	12.8%	NA
1975	8.6	8.4	10.2	13.2%
1980	8.8	9.2	6.9	16.5
1985	7.0	7.1	6.5	14.5
1988	6.7	7.1	6.0	19.6
18-19				
1970	16.2	14.1	31.2	NA
1975	16.0	14.7	25.4	30.1
1980	15.7	14.9	21.2	39.0
1985	14.3	13.8	17.3	30.6
1988	14.6	14.3	17.9	31.2
20-21				
1970	16.6	14.6	29.6	NA
1975	16.6	14.8	28.7	31.6
1980	15.9	14.5	24.8	41.6
1985	13.9	13.4	17.7	27.9
1988	14.6	14.2	18.2	43.2
22-24				
1970	18.7	16.3	37.8	NA
1975	14.5	12.6	27.8	41.7
1980	15.2	13.9	24.0	40.6
1985	14.1	13.3	17.8	33.9
1988	14.6	14.1	17.2	42.5

*Persons of Latino origin can be of any race.

NA — Data not available.

Sources: U.S. Department of Commerce, Bureau of the Census, *Current Population Reports*, Series P-20, No. 222, School Enrollment: October 1970 (1971), Table 1; U.S. Department of Commerce, Bureau of the Census, *Current Population Reports*, Series P-20, No. 303, School Enrollment—Social and Economic Characteristics of Students: October 1975 (1976), Table 1; U.S. Department of Commerce, Bureau of the Census, *Current Population Reports*, Series P-20, No. 400, School Enrollment—Social and Economic Characteristics of Students: October 1981 and October 1980 (1985), Table 26; U.S. Department of Commerce, Bureau of the Census, *Current Population Reports*, Series P-20, No. 426, School Enrollment—Social and Economic Characteristics of Students: October 1985 and 1984 (1988), Table 1; and U.S. Department of Commerce, Bureau of the Census, *Current Population Reports*, Series P-20, No. 443, School Enrollment—Social and Economic Characteristics of Students: October 1988 and 1987 (1990), Table 1.

Table 4.18

School Completion Status, by Race and Latino Origin, and Age, 1988 (Percent of Age Group)

School Completion Status, Age	Total	White	Black	Latino*
Enrolled below college				
18-19	13.9%	11.7%	23.7%	16.3%
20-21	0.6	0.7	0.3	2.0
High school graduate				
18-19	71.5	74.0	58.4	52.3
20-21	84.8	85.1	81.5	54.9
Dropout				
18-19	14.6	14.3	17.9	31.2
20-21	14.6	14.2	18.2	43.2

*Persons of Latino origin can be of any race.

Source: U.S. Department of Commerce, Bureau of the Census, *Current Population Reports*, Series P-20, No. 443, School Enrollment—Social and Economic Characteristics of Students: October 1988 and 1987 (1990), Table 1. Calculations by Children's Defense Fund.

Fig. 4.6

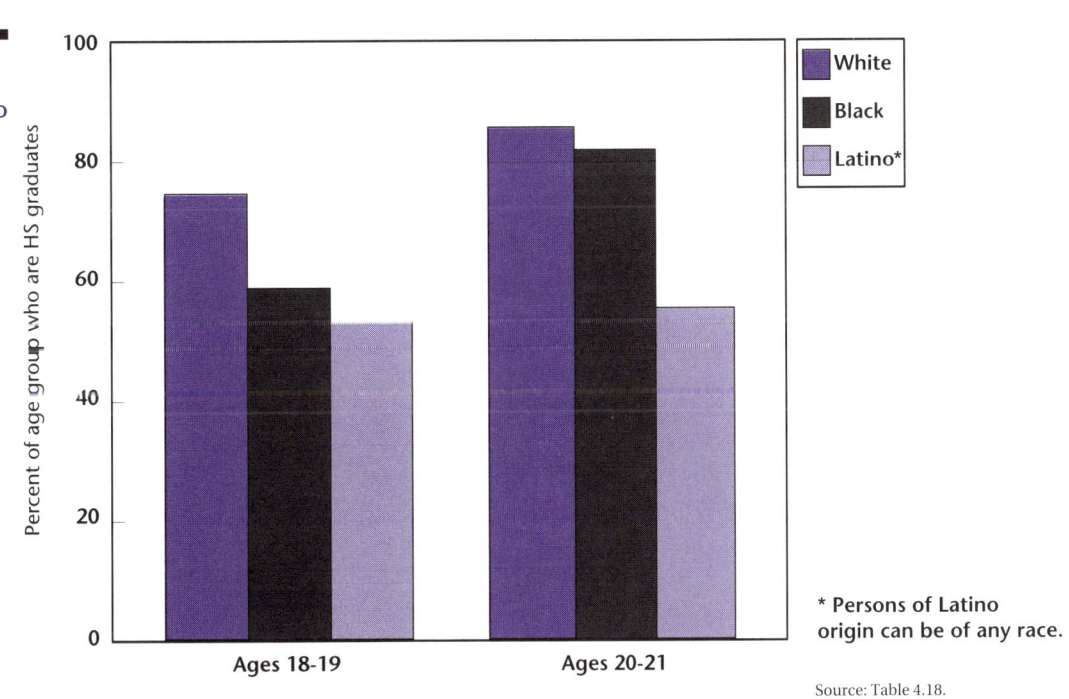

High School Graduation Rates, by Race and Latino Origin and Age, 1988

* Persons of Latino origin can be of any race.

Source: Table 4.18.

THE ADOLESCENT AND YOUNG ADULT FACT BOOK

Table 4.19

School Enrollment and Educational Attainment Among 20- and 21-Year-Olds, by Race and Poverty Status, 1987 (Percent)

Poverty Status, Enrollment, Attainment	Total	White	Black
All income levels			
Enrolled	35.8%	36.0%	29.0%
Not enrolled	63.9	63.7	71.0
High school graduate	88.0	89.1	80.9
Dropout	11.0	10.2	17.4
Poor			
Enrolled	27.0	24.9	21.7
Not enrolled	72.9	74.6	78.3
High school graduate	71.1	70.7	67.5
Dropout	27.7	28.1	30.0
Not poor			
Enrolled	37.1	37.2	31.5
Not enrolled	62.6	62.4	68.5
High school graduate	90.4	91.1	85.3
Dropout	8.6	8.1	13.2

Note: Enrolled and Not enrolled may not add to 100% because of rounding.

Source: U.S. Department of Commerce, Bureau of the Census, unpublished tabulations from the March 1988 Current Population Survey. Calculations by Children's Defense Fund.

Table 4.20

Dropout Rates Among 16- to 24-Year-Olds, by Race and Latino Origin, and by Metropolitan Status, 1988 (Percent Not Enrolled, Not High School Graduate)

Metropolitan Status	Total	White	Black	Latino*
Total	12.9%	12.7%	14.9%	35.8%
Central city	16.1	16.1	16.8	37.1
Suburban	10.5	10.8	9.1	34.7
Non-metropolitan	13.0	12.5	17.0	30.4

*Persons of Latino origin can be of any race.

Source: U.S. Department of Commerce, Bureau of the Census, *Current Population Reports*, Series P-20, No. 443, School Enrollment—Social and Economic Characteristics of Students: October 1988 and 1987 (1990), Tables 1 and 2. Calculations by Children's Defense Fund.

Table 4.21

College Attainment Among 18- to 21-Year-Old High School Graduates, by Race and Poverty Status, 1975 and 1987 (Percent With Some College)

Year, Poverty Status	Total	White	Black
1975			
All	33.6%	33.9%	28.4%
Poor	33.8	33.4	30.7
Nonpoor	33.6	33.9	27.8
1987			
All	38.7	39.6	30.8
Poor	27.6	29.6	18.7
Nonpoor	40.2	40.7	34.8

Sources: U.S. Department of Commerce, Bureau of the Census, *Current Population Reports*, Series P-60, No. 106, Characteristics of the Population Below the Poverty Level: 1975 (1977), Table 13; and U.S. Department of Commerce, Bureau of the Census, *Current Population Reports*, Series P-60, No. 163, Poverty in the United States: 1987 (1989), Table 9. Calculations by Children's Defense Fund.

Table 4.22

Trends in Highest Degree Attained Four Years After High School, by Race and Latino Origin and by Socioeconomic Status (SES), 1972-1982 (Percent Attaining Each Credential)

High School Class, Attainment	Total	White	Black	Latino*	SES Low	SES High
1972						
No high school diploma	1.0%	0.7%	2.3%	4.1%	1.6%	0.4%
High school diploma	53.2	52.5	54.9	59.4	63.8	42.5
Postsecondary certificate	21.3	20.7	24.2	25.7	22.4	17.1
Associate's degree	9.1	9.6	7.4	6.5	6.5	9.1
Bachelor's degree	15.4	16.6	11.2	4.3	5.6	30.8
1980						
No high school diploma	1.2	0.9	2.9	2.2	1.5	0.0
High school diploma	75.1	74.6	78.1	79.0	80.9	69.7
Postsecondary certificate	10.2	10.0	11.2	9.9	10.6	7.3
Associate's degree	6.4	6.6	4.6	7.0	5.0	7.1
Bachelor's degree	7.1	8.0	3.2	1.9	1.9	15.9
1982						
No high school diploma	2.6	1.8	4.1	5.4	4.5	0.7
High school diploma	77.6	77.0	79.8	79.7	81.0	73.1
Postsecondary certificate	7.3	7.1	9.1	7.9	9.0	5.3
Associate's degree	5.5	6.0	3.5	5.1	4.1	5.2
Bachelor's degree	7.1	8.3	3.3	1.9	1.4	15.7

*Persons of Latino origin can be of any race.

Source: U.S. Department of Education, National Center for Education Statistics, *Changes in Educational Attainment: A Comparison Among 1972, 1980, and 1982 High School Seniors* (1989), pp. 14, 16, 18-19.

THE ADOLESCENT AND YOUNG ADULT FACT BOOK

Table 4.23

Trends in Postsecondary Attainment Four Years After High School, by Type of High School and by Academic Program, 1972-1982 (Percent Receiving Each Credential)

High School Class, Attainment	Type of High School Public	Type of High School Private	Academic Program Academic	Academic Program General	Academic Program Vocational
1972					
No high school diploma	1.0%	0.3%	0.3%	1.6%	1.4%
High school diploma	53.9	43.3	40.6	60.9	64.8
Postsecondary certificate	21.1	21.2	17.1	23.7	25.3
Associate's degree	9.2	8.4	12.2	7.1	6.6
Bachelor's degree	14.7	26.8	29.8	6.7	2.0
1980					
No high school diploma	1.4	0.0	0.1	0.9	0.9
High school diploma	75.5	72.4	70.5	78.6	77.4
Postsecondary certificate	10.4	8.2	7.8	10.6	14.1
Associate's degree	6.4	5.9	7.3	6.2	6.5
Bachelor's degree	6.3	13.5	14.4	3.7	1.1
1982					
No high school diploma	2.8	0.3	0.7	4.1	4.1
High school diploma	78.2	72.9	73.6	80.8	80.5
Postsecondary certificate	7.4	6.1	6.3	7.6	8.8
Associate's degree	5.4	5.9	5.9	5.1	5.2
Bachelor's degree	6.2	14.8	13.4	2.3	1.5

Sources: U.S. Department of Education, National Center for Education Statistics, *Changes in Educational Attainment: A Comparison Among 1972, 1980, and 1982 High School Seniors* (1989), p. 20; and U.S. Department of Education, National Center for Education Statistics, unpublished tabulations (1988).

EMPLOYMENT, EARNINGS, AND INCOME

America faces a serious youth employment problem. Many high school- or college-age youths work to supplement their families' incomes, have left school early to join the labor force, are on their own, or have families of their own to support. But because of changes in the labor market, decent-paying jobs increasingly require higher education or specialized job skills that many young people have not had enough opportunity to gain. As a result, youths without education beyond high school are finding it difficult or impossible to find stable, full-time work that pays enough to support a family. Minorities and women are at greatest risk of unemployment, only part time (or sporadic) employment, and low earnings.

Employment

In 1989 almost half of both males and females ages 16 to 19 had jobs. Among youths ages 20 to 24, nearly three-fourths of all males and two-thirds of all females were working. About 15 percent of the teenagers and between 8 and 9 percent of the young adults in the labor force (either working or looking for work) are officially unemployed. (Technically, an "unemployed" person is someone who is not employed and is looking for work.)

These figures represent a slight drop in the proportion of males with jobs since 1973, and a significant rise in the proportion of females with jobs. Males are still more likely than females to be employed, however.

Regardless of gender or age, black youths are the most likely to be unemployed (in 1989 about 32 percent among 16- to 19-year-olds, and 18 percent among 20- to 24-year-olds). Latino youths were not as likely to be unemployed, although their unemployment rates were high (about 19 percent among teens, and from 10 to 12 percent among young adults). Whites had the lowest unemployment rates (14 percent among male teens, 12 percent among female teens, and about 7 percent among young adults).

Education is a major predictor of employment, regardless of the young person's age, race, or gender. Among all 16- to 24-year-olds not enrolled in school, the proportion with jobs increases steadily with increasing education, from 52 percent among high school dropouts to 90 percent among college graduates. At equivalent levels of education, however, blacks and Latinos generally are less likely than their white peers to be employed.

Many young people, especially females, work only part time. About half of all employed teens and about 15 percent of 20- to 24-year-olds voluntarily work part time, although a sizable proportion, especially among blacks, are forced to work part time because they cannot find full-time jobs. Black young adults, both males and females, are about twice as likely as their white counterparts to be unable to obtain full-time work.

Many older teens and young adults enter the military instead of civilian employment. Black youths are about 50 percent more likely than white youths to be in the military, regardless of gender.

Earnings and income

Over the decade of the 1980s, young workers' earnings actually declined after accounting for inflation. Young men's earnings were particularly affected; they experienced an overall drop of almost 20 percent from 1979 to 1989. The decline was worse for minority men than for white men. Young women's earnings also declined over this period, but not by as much (between 5 and 9 percent). (Interestingly, as pointed out in the chapter on Sexual Activity, Childbearing, and Family Formation, the proportion of young people marrying declined over the same period of time.) Young workers also lost ground compared with older workers.

Gender is one of the biggest factors affecting young people's earnings. On average, a female year-round, full-time worker with some high school education earns less than a male with no high school education; a female with at least some college education earns only slightly more than a male high school graduate with no college education.

Regardless of race, Latino origin, or gender, however, young full-time, year-round workers' earnings increase with increasing education. In 1987 mean annual earnings among young males ranged from $11,043 for those with no high school education to $17,523 for those with at least some college education. Among females, mean annual earnings ranged from $8,420 for those with no high school education to $14,967 for those with at least some college education.

More than three-fourths of all youths receive earnings from employment. In contrast, only one in 100 young men and one in 20 young women receive income from welfare benefits. Yet a significant proportion of youths receive at least part of their income from sources other than wages and salaries, including self-employment, property (interest and dividends), disability payments, and welfare. Males are more likely than females to be self-employed or to receive veterans', unemployment, or workers' compensation. Females, on the other hand, are more likely to receive income from interest or dividends, disability payments, welfare, or alimony or child support. About 3 million children ages 10 to 18 and almost 1.2 million mothers younger than 26—including about 40,000 younger than 18—receive welfare benefits. These mothers younger than 26 account for only 35 percent of all adult women receiving AFDC benefits.

Table 5.1

Trends in the Employment–Population Ratio of Adolescents and Young Adults, by Race and Latino Origin, Age, and Gender, 1973-1989 (Percent of Population)

Age, Gender, Year	Total	White	Black	Latino*
16-19				
Male				
1973	51.4%	54.3%	32.8%	NA
1979	51.7	55.7	28.7	NA
1983	43.1	47.4	20.4	37.6%
1989	48.7	52.6	30.4	44.9
Female				
1973	40.5	43.6	22.0	NA
1979	45.3	49.4	22.4	NA
1983	40.0	44.5	17.0	27.1
1989	46.4	50.5	27.1	33.3
20-24				
Male				
1973	79.0	80.2	72.6	NA
1979	78.9	81.1	65.5	NA
1983	71.3	74.3	54.5	71.4
1989	77.8	80.2	65.8	81.7
Female				
1973	56.0	57.4	47.4	NA
1979	62.4	65.0	47.7	NA
1983	60.9	64.7	40.3	47.3
1989	66.4	69.0	53.7	53.3

*Persons of Latino origin can be of any race.
NA — Data not available.

Source: U.S. Department of Labor, Bureau of Labor Statistics, *Handbook of Labor Statistics*, Bulletin 2340 (1989), Table 16; U.S. Department of Labor, Bureau of Labor Statistics, *Employment and Earnings*, Vol. 37, No. 1 (January 1990), Table 3; and U.S. Department of Labor, Bureau of Labor Statistics, unpublished tabulations. Calculations by Children's Defense Fund.

Fig. 5.1

The Employment–Population Ratio of Adolescents and Young Adults, by Age, Race and Latino Origin, and Gender, 1989

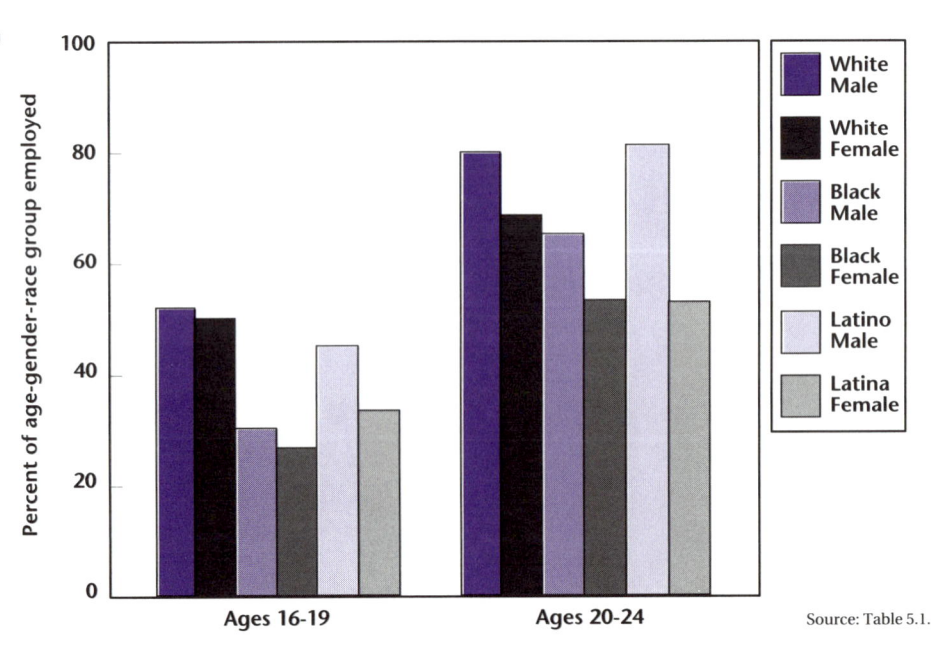

Source: Table 5.1.

Table 5.2

Trends in the Unemployment Rate of Adolescents and Young Adults, by Race and Latino Origin, Age, and Gender, 1973-1989 (Percent of Labor Force)

Age, Gender, Year	Total	White	Black	Latino*
16-19				
Male				
1973	13.9%	12.3%	27.8%	NA
1979	15.9	13.9	34.2	NA
1983	23.3	20.2	48.8	28.7%
1989	15.9	13.7	31.9	20.2
Female				
1973	15.3	13.0	36.1	NA
1979	16.4	14.0	39.1	NA
1983	21.3	18.3	48.2	28.0
1989	14.0	11.5	33.0	18.2
20-24				
Male				
1973	7.3	6.6	13.2	NA
1979	8.7	7.5	18.7	NA
1983	15.9	13.8	31.4	17.0
1989	8.8	7.5	17.9	9.7
Female				
1973	8.5	7.1	18.4	NA
1979	9.6	7.8	22.6	NA
1983	12.9	10.3	31.8	16.2
1989	8.3	6.8	18.1	12.2

*Persons of Latino origin can be of any race.
NA — Data not available.

Source: U.S. Department of Labor, Bureau of Labor Statistics, *Handbook of Labor Statistics*, Bulletin 2340 (1989), Table 28; U.S. Department of Labor, Bureau of Labor Statistics, *Employment and Earnings*, Vol. 37, No. 1 (January 1990), Table 3; and U.S. Department of Labor, Bureau of Labor Statistics, unpublished tabulations. Calculations by Children's Defense Fund.

Fig. 5.2

The Unemployment Rate of Adolescents and Young Adults, by Age, Race and Latino Origin, and Gender, 1989

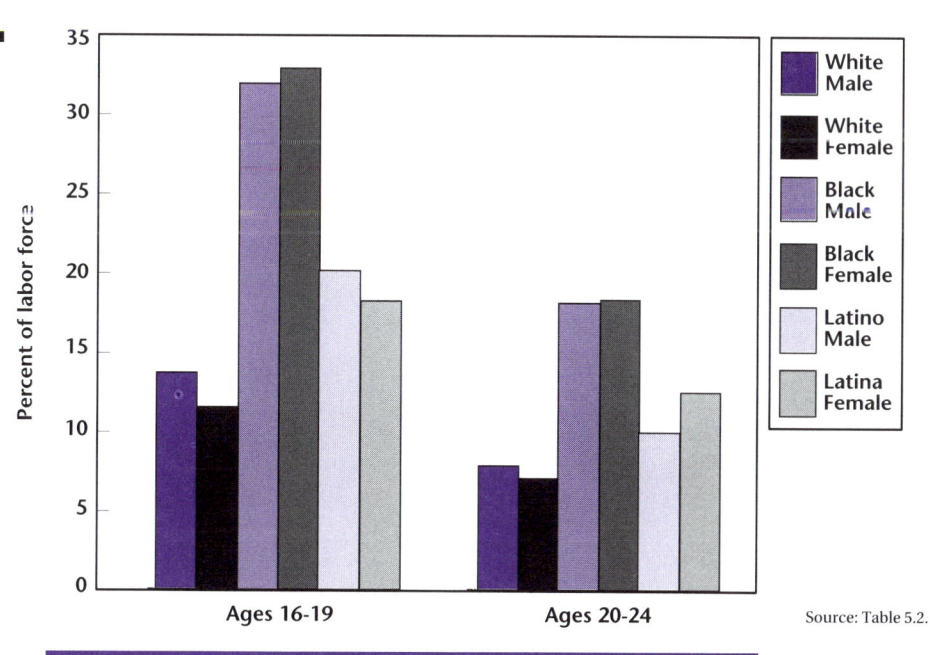

Source: Table 5.2.

Table 5.3

Employment Status of Adolescents and Young Adults, by Race and Latino Origin, School Enrollment Status, and Age, 1989 (Percent)

Enrollment Status, Age, Employment Status	Total	White	Black	Latino*
Enrolled				
16-19				
Employed	39.0%	42.7%	22.1%	27.2%
Looking for work	6.0	5.5	9.4	6.8
20-24				
Employed	56.0	58.0	45.9	58.8
Looking for work	4.0	3.6	7.0	4.5
Not enrolled				
16-19				
Employed	60.9	65.2	39.5	53.2
Looking for work	12.1	10.5	20.9	12.6
20-24				
Employed	76.6	79.4	62.0	69.4
Looking for work	7.6	6.4	14.2	8.7

*Persons of Latino origin can be of any race.

Source: U.S. Department of Labor, Bureau of Labor Statistics, *Employment and Earnings*, Vol. 37, No. 1 (January 1990), Table 6. Calculations by Children's Defense Fund.

Table 5.4

Employment Status of Adolescents and Young Adults Ages 16 to 24 Not Enrolled in School, by Race and Latino Origin and Educational Attainment, 1989 (Percent)

Educational Attainment, Employment Status	Total	White	Black	Latino*
Not high school graduate				
Employed	52.2%	56.5%	31.9%	56.2%
Looking for work	12.9	11.5	20.4	10.6
High school graduate				
Employed	75.8	79.1	59.7	71.6
Looking for work	8.5	6.9	16.5	9.3
Some college				
Employed	84.9	86.1	79.3	80.6
Looking for work	5.4	4.7	9.6	7.7
College graduate				
Employed	90.4	91.2	87.8	82.7
Looking for work	4.8	4.6	6.1	9.6

*Persons of Latino origin can be of any race.

Source: U.S. Department of Labor, Bureau of Labor Statistics, *Employment and Earnings*, Vol. 37, No. 1 (January 1990), Table 6. Calculations by Children's Defense Fund.

Fig. 5.3

Employment–Population Ratio of Youths Ages 16 to 24 Not Enrolled in School, by Race and Latino Origin and Educational Attainment, 1989

*Persons of Latino origin can be of any race.

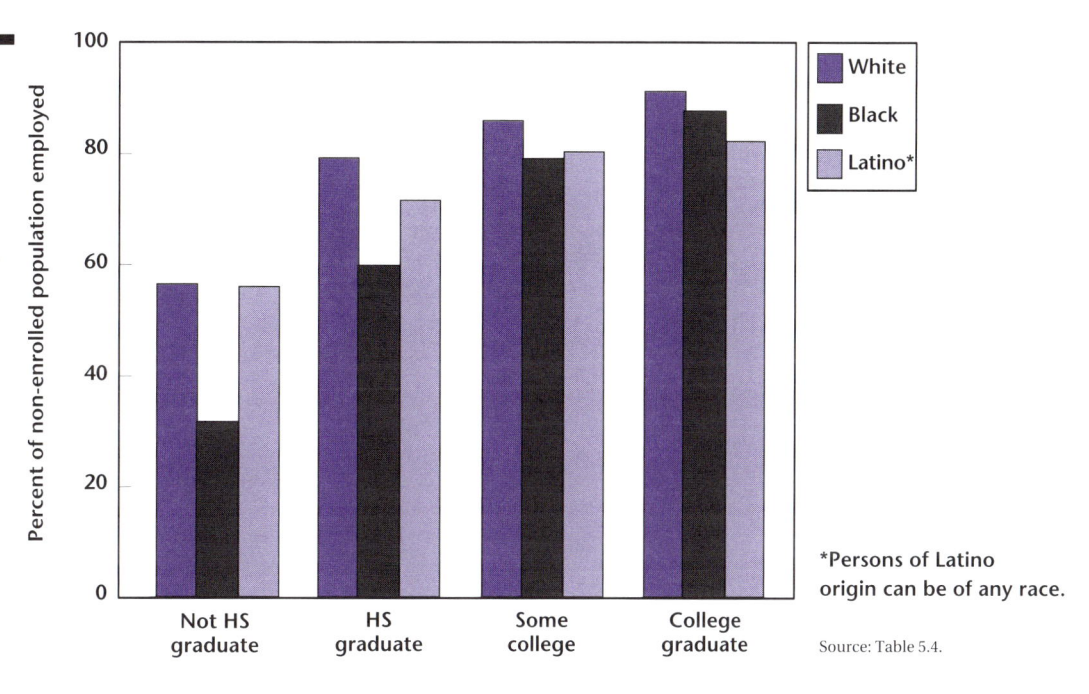

Source: Table 5.4.

Table 5.5

Full-Time Employment Status of Adolescents and Young Adults, by Race, Gender, and Age, 1989 (Percent of Those Employed Who Work Full Time)

Gender, Age	Total	White	Black
Male			
16-19	41.0%	41.6%	36.7%
20-24	80.5	81.1	78.5
Female			
16-19	31.3	31.7	30.8
20-24	71.9	71.9	73.1

Source: U.S. Department of Labor, Bureau of Labor Statistics, *Employment and Earnings*, Vol. 37, No. 1 (January 1990), Table 7. Calculations by Children's Defense Fund.

THE ADOLESCENT AND YOUNG ADULT FACT BOOK

Table 5.6

Reasons for Working Part Time Among Adolescents and Young Adults, by Race, Age, and Gender, 1989 (Percent of Those Employed)

Age, Gender, Reason	Total	White	Black
16-19			
Male			
Voluntary	49.9%	50.1%	47.4%
Economic reasons, usually full time	2.1	2.0	3.4
Economic reasons, usually part time	7.0	6.3	12.5
Female			
Voluntary	59.8	59.6	57.2
Economic reasons, usually full time	1.5	1.5	1.3
Economic reasons, usually part time	7.4	7.2	10.0
20-24			
Male			
Voluntary	13.4	13.4	10.9
Economic reasons, usually full time	2.3	2.3	3.0
Economic reasons, usually part time	3.7	3.2	7.7
Female			
Voluntary	21.7	22.3	16.8
Economic reasons, usually full time	1.7	1.6	2.2
Economic reasons, usually part time	4.7	4.3	7.9

Note: "Economic reasons" means "cannot find full-time employment." All persons working part time for economic reasons want to work full time. Prior employment of some of them is "usually full time," and of the others "usually part time."

Source: U.S. Department of Labor, Bureau of Labor Statistics, *Employment and Earnings*, Vol. 37, No. 1 (January 1990), Table 7. Calculations by Children's Defense Fund.

Table 5.7

Percent of Population on Active Military Duty, by Race, Gender, and Age, June 1988

Gender, Age	Total	White	Black	Other
Both genders				
Under 20	2.5%	2.3%	3.2%	3.1%
20-24	3.7	3.4	5.4	5.3
Male				
Under 20	4.4	4.2	5.5	5.3
20-24	6.6	6.0	9.2	9.1
Female				
Under 20	0.5	0.4	0.9	0.6
20-24	0.8	0.7	1.7	1.2

Source: Unpublished tabulations from the U.S. Department of Defense; and U.S. Department of Commerce, Bureau of the Census, *Current Population Reports*, Series P-25, No. 1045, United States Population Estimates, by Age, Sex, Race, and Hispanic Origin: 1980 to 1988 (1990), Table 1. Calculations by Children's Defense Fund.

Table 5.8

Median Weekly Earnings of 16- to 24-Year-Old Full-Time Wage and Salary Workers, by Race and Latino Origin and by Gender, 1979-1989

Gender, Year	Total	White	Black	Latino*
Male				
1979	$196	$199	$167	$181
1989	271	276	228	236
Change in real dollars	-19.0%	-18.8%	-20.1%	-23.7%
Female				
1979	$154	$155	$144	$139
1989	246	248	224	225
Change in real dollars	-6.5%	-6.3%	-8.9%	-5.2%

*Persons of Latino origin can be of any race.

Sources: U.S. Department of Labor, Bureau of Labor Statistics, *Handbook of Labor Statistics*, Bulletin 2340 (1989), Table 41; U.S. Department of Labor, Bureau of Labor Statistics, unpublished annual averages from the Current Population Survey (1980 and 1990); and U.S. Department of Labor, Bureau of Labor Statistics, *CPI Detailed Report: January 1991* (1991), Table 24. Calculations by Children's Defense Fund.

Table 5.9

Median Weekly Earnings of Full-Time Workers Ages 16 to 24 as a Percent of Earnings of Full-Time Workers Ages 25 and Older, by Race and Latino Origin and by Gender, 1979-1989

Gender, Year	Total	White	Black	Latino*
Male				
1979	62.4%	62.0%	68.2%	84.2%
1989	54.2	53.9	60.3	67.6
Female				
1979	79.4	78.7	81.4	83.2
1989	70.1	69.5	71.6	79.2

*Persons of Latino origin can be of any race.

Source: U.S. Department of Labor, Bureau of Labor Statistics, *Handbook of Labor Statistics*, Bulletin 2340 (1989), Table 41; and U.S. Department of Labor, Bureau of Labor Statistics, unpublished annual averages from the Current Population Survey (1980 and 1990). Calculations by Children's Defense Fund.

Table 5.10

Annual Earnings of Young Adults Ages 18 to 24, by Race and Latino Origin, Employment Status, Gender, and Educational Attainment, 1987 (Mean Earnings)

Employment Status, Gender, Educational Attainment	Total	White	Black	Latino*
All workers				
Male				
No high school	$ 7,063	$ 7,404	—	$ 7,197
Some high school	6,030	6,454	$ 3,530	6,389
High school graduate	10,039	10,355	8,202	9,775
Any college	9,375	9,482	8,964	10,372
Female				
No high school	5,336	5,050	—	5,395
Some high school	3,752	3,809	3,749	4,114
High school graduate	7,274	7,489	5,802	7,398
Any college	8,235	8,348	7,249	9,594
Year-round, full-time workers				
Male				
No high school	11,043	11,243	—	9,791
Some high school	12,297	12,485	—	10,360
High school graduate	14,732	15,056	12,293	13,665
Any college	17,523	17,453	17,928	15,307
Female				
No high school	8,420	—	—	—
Some high school	10,301	10,659	—	—
High school graduate	12,180	12,253	11,634	12,117
Any college	14,967	15,007	14,285	15,189

*Persons of Latino origin can be of any race.
— Sample number too small to calculate a reliable income figure.

Source: U.S. Department of Commerce, Bureau of the Census, *Current Population Reports*, Series P-60, No. 162, Money Income of Households, Families, and Persons in the United States: 1987 (1989), Table 36.

Table 5.11

Annual Income of Young Adults Ages 18 to 24 Who Work Full Time, Year-Round, by Race and Latino Origin, Gender, and Marital Status, 1987 (Median Income)

Gender, Marital Status	Total	White	Black	Latino*
Male				
Single	$12,999	$13,312	$11,300	$11,119
Married, spouse present	16,294	16,297	—	12,256
Divorced	14,770	—	—	—
Female				
Single	12,385	12,330	12,615	11,506
Married, spouse present	12,719	12,806	12,279	12,035
Divorced	12,436	12,296	—	—

*Persons of Latino origin can be of any race.
— Sample number too small to calculate a reliable income figure.

Source: U.S. Department of Commerce, Bureau of the Census, *Current Population Reports*, Series P-60, No. 162, Money Income of Households, Families, and Persons in the United States: 1987 (1989), Table 33.

Table 5.12

Sources of Income Among Youths Ages 15 to 24, by Gender, 1987 (Percent Receiving Each Type of Income)

Source	Male	Female
Wages, salaries	82.9%	76.2%
Self-employment	6.9	2.6
Property*	77.7	94.4
Supplemental Security Income	3.0	6.7
Public assistance, welfare	1.0	5.5
Veterans', unemployment, workers' compensation	8.8	4.8
Alimony, child support	0.2	1.8

*Includes interest, dividends, rental income.

Source: U.S. Department of Commerce, Bureau of the Census, *Current Population Reports*, Series P-60, No. 162, Money Income of Households, Families, and Persons in the United States: 1987 (1989), Tables 34 and 30. Calculations by Children's Defense Fund.

Table 5.13

Adolescent and Young Adult AFDC Recipients, by Gender, AFDC Status, and Age, 1988

AFDC Status, Age	Male	Female
Recipient children		
10-14	811,577	800,460
15-18	667,707	662,198
Recipient adults		
11-17	7,997	39,835
18-19	8,397	189,218
20-21	9,197	288,806
22-25	45,584	663,921

Note: Recipient adults are usually parents.

Source: U.S. Department of Health and Human Services, Family Support Administration, Office of Family Assistance, *Characteristics and Financial Circumstances of AFDC Recipients, FY 1988* (1990), Tables 18, 19, 20, and 24. Calculations by Children's Defense Fund.

SEXUAL ACTIVITY, PREGNANCY, AND FAMILY FORMATION

Every 64 seconds—about the time it takes for an average person to leave the house, get in a car, and back out of the driveway—a baby is born to a teenage mother in this country. Five minutes later, a baby will have been born to a teenager who already has a child. Ten hours later, by the time this person perhaps returns home from work, more than 560 babies will have been born to teenagers in America.

Adolescent pregnancy, which for too many young people begins or perpetuates a cycle of poverty, remains a crisis in America. After rising steadily during the 1970s, estimated adolescent pregnancy and abortion rates leveled off during the first half of the 1980s. Still, teens ages 15 to 19 account for an estimated 1 million pregnancies each year. Those younger than 15 account for an estimated 30,000 pregnancies each year. An alarming one in every eight births in this country is to a teenager. As might be expected, the vast majority of these teen births are unwanted or mistimed.

Although there are more white than minority teen pregnancies, minority teens have higher pregnancy rates. In 1988 one in 10 white births was to a teenager, compared with one in six Latino births, and more than one in five black births.

Sexual activity and pregnancy

The immediate causes of too-early pregnancy are obvious enough: Adolescents are increasingly likely to be sexually experienced, and only a fraction of sexually active teens use contraception.

In 1988 half of all unmarried girls ages 15 to 19 were sexually experienced (double the proportion in 1970). About three-fourths of all 18- and 19-year-old girls are sexually active, regardless of race or ethnic background. Blacks, both male and female, become sexually active an average of one to two years earlier than either whites or Latinos, and males become sexually active at younger ages than females. Of all youths, black males are the most likely to begin sexual activity at a young age: About 30 percent of black boys younger than 14 have had sexual intercourse, three or four times the rate among Latino and white males their age, and several times the rate among girls their age.

More than one-third of all teenage girls used no contraception at first intercourse. Among sexually active black and Latina teens, almost half used no contraception at first intercourse. Among those who did use contraception, the most common method was condoms.

Childbearing

The number of births to teens peaked in 1970 at 656,000 and declined to about 490,000 in 1988. The number of births to girls younger than 15 also has declined: from about 12,000 a year in the early and mid-1970s to about 10,000 a year throughout the 1980s.

However, birth rates among unmarried teens continue to climb. The increase has occurred mainly among whites; the rates among blacks have changed very little. By 1988 more than 322,000 births—almost two-thirds of all births to teens—were to unmarried girls, five times the ratio in 1950.

The roots of too-early pregnancy and childbirth run deep. The link between teen pregnancy and educational difficulties, especially among minorities, is well documented. In 1988 more than half of the black and Latina women ages 18 to 24 who were not high school graduates were mothers. While teen mothers are about as likely as other teens to complete high school eventually, they may take longer, and they are more likely to get a GED (General Equivalency Diploma). They also are more likely to end their education with completion of high school.

In addition, lack of close contact with adult role models, peer pressure, family poverty, a perception among many teens that there are few opportunities for success open to them, and insufficient sexuality and contraception education all contribute to teen pregnancy and childbirth.

However the specific factors play out for each young parent and baby, the resulting cycle of negative outcomes often lasts for years, if not a lifetime. For many the troubles begin before the baby is born, with lack of prenatal care, one of the best assurances of an infant's health. Teenagers are more likely than older mothers to receive late or no prenatal care and to have babies with low birthweight, a strong predictor of later health problems. In 1988 only slightly more than half of the births to teens were to women who received early prenatal care.

The problems continue after the baby is born. Recent changes in the labor market have made it extremely hard for young parents—especially single mothers—to support a family. Jobs that don't require much education or specialized skills, yet pay enough to support a family, have all but disappeared. The mean annual earnings among young workers with no high school education are $11,043 for men and $8,420 for women for full-time, year-round work. Among those who have finished high school but received no college education, the mean annual earnings are $14,732 for men and $12,180 for women. A large fraction of young people, especially minorities, cannot find jobs at all.

Low earnings and high unemployment rates mean that teen families seldom can make it financially without outside help. Moreover, the vast majority of teen families are headed by single mothers, which not only means there is no possibility of a second income from a spouse, but there is the added expense of child care while the mother works. Even parents who manage to find free or inexpensive child care rarely have the means to provide for the family's most basic needs.

Marriage and cohabitation

In 1989 the median ages at first marriage among Americans were about 26 for men and 24 among women. Despite a common perception that the more youthful marriages of the 1950s represent the historical norm in America, they actually were an aberration. The current median ages of first marriage for men and women are about the same as they were from 1890 through the early twentieth century. The ages dropped slightly over the next few decades, but did not dip significantly—to about 23 for men and 20 for women—until the 1950s. In the 1970s the trend began shifting back to later marriage.

At every age, young females are more likely to have married than their male peers. Latinos are more likely than whites or blacks to have married, regardless of age or gender. Blacks, on the other hand, are less likely than whites or Latinos to have married. About one-third of all young adult women have cohabited, and white women are somewhat more likely than black women to have cohabited.

Table 6.1

Trends in Sexual Initiation Among Unmarried Women Ages 15 to 19, 1970-1988 (Percent Sexually Experienced)

Year	Percent of Unmarried Women
1970	25%
1975	34
1980	40
1984	43
1988	50

Source: National Research Council, *Risking the Future: Adolescent Sexuality, Pregnancy, and Childbearing*, Volume II (1987), Table 3.1; and Jacqueline Darroch Forrest and Susheela Singh, The Sexual and Reproductive Behavior of American Women, 1982-1988, *Family Planning Perspectives*, Vol. 22, No. 5 (September/October 1990), Table 3.

Table 6.2

Age of Initiation of Sexual Intercourse, by Race and Latino Origin and Gender, and Age of Women At First Pregnancy, 1983-1984 (Cumulative Percent)

Event, Gender, Age	Total	White	Black	Latino*
First sexual intercourse				
Male				
Under 14	10.2%	6.8%	30.4%	9.9%
14	17.2	12.5	44.3	18.3
15	29.1	23.5	61.4	31.8
16	48.4	43.3	78.6	49.9
17	64.8	60.8	87.3	68.0
18	78.2	75.5	93.5	80.3
19 or older	92.0	91.2	96.8	91.6
Female				
Under 14	3.3	3.2	4.9	2.0
14	8.5	7.9	12.5	6.1
15	17.6	16.6	24.2	15.2
16	33.2	31.3	45.7	28.5
17	50.9	49.2	64.2	42.3
18	67.6	66.3	79.1	58.4
19 or older	89.1	88.7	93.1	84.6
First pregnancy				
Female				
Under 14	0.7	0.5	1.6	0.7
14	2.1	1.4	5.8	2.3
15	5.6	4.2	13.2	6.9
16	10.9	8.3	23.6	15.3
17	17.4	14.3	33.0	23.0
18	25.4	22.0	41.3	33.4
19 or older	50.5	47.0	65.4	61.7

*Persons of Latino origin can be of any race.

Source: Frank L. Mott and R. Jean Haurin, *The Inter-Relatedness of Age at First Intercourse, Early Pregnancy, Alcohol, and Drug Use Among American Adolescents*, Center for Human Resource Research, The Ohio State University (1987), Table 1.

Table 6.3

Sexual Activity Among Women Ages 15 to 19, by Race and Latino Origin, and by Age, 1988 (Percent Sexually Experienced)

Age	Total	White Non-Latina	Black Non-Latina	Latina*
15-19	53.2	52.4	60.8	48.5
15-17	38.4	36.2	50.5	36.1
18-19	74.4	74.3	78.0	70.0

*Women of Latino origin can be of any race.

Source: Jacqueline Darroch Forrest and Susheela Singh, The Sexual and Reproductive Behavior of American Women, 1982-1988, *Family Planning Perspectives*, Vol. 22, No. 5 (September/October 1990), Table 4.

Table 6.4

Contraceptive Use At First Intercourse Among Women Ages 15 to 19, by Race and Latino Origin, and by Method Used, 1988 (Percent)

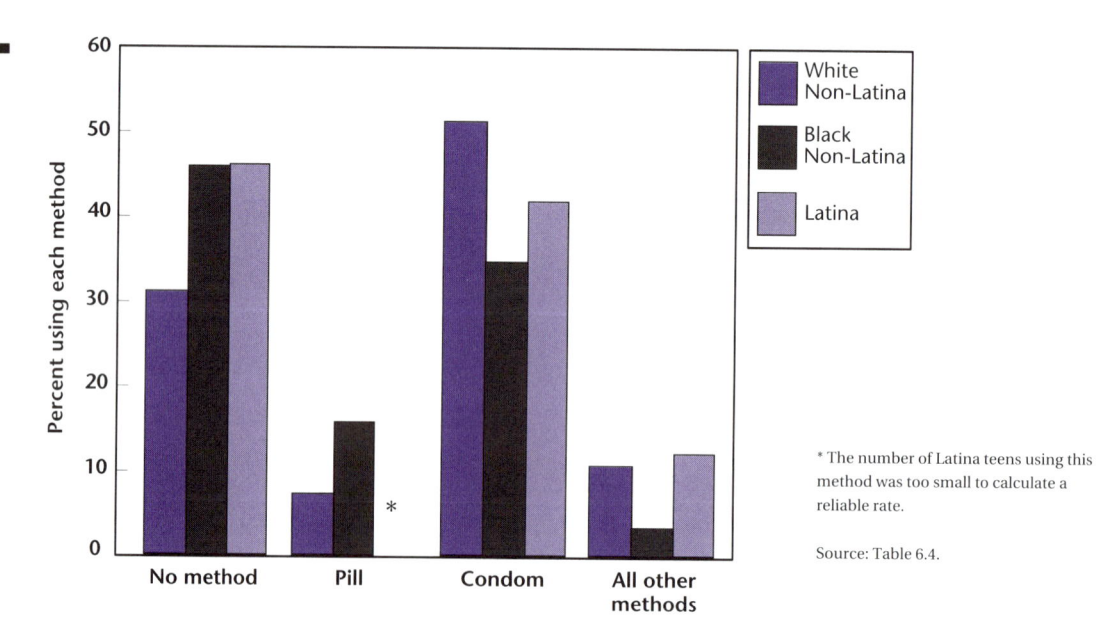

Method	Total	White Non-Latina	Black Non-Latina	Latina*
None	35.0%	31.0%	45.9%	46.1%
Any method	65.0	69.0	54.1	53.9
Pill	8.2	7.1	15.7	—
Condom	47.4	51.1	34.8	41.8
Withdrawal	8.4	9.6	—	—

*Women of Latino origin can be of any race.
— Number too small to calculate a reliable rate.

Source: Jacqueline Darroch Forrest and Susheela Singh, The Sexual and Reproductive Behavior of American Women, 1982-1988, *Family Planning Perspectives*, Vol. 22, No. 5 (September/October 1990), Table 5.

Fig. 6.1

Contraceptive Use At First Intercourse Among Women Ages 15 to 19, by Race and Latino Origin, and by Method Used, 1988

* The number of Latina teens using this method was too small to calculate a reliable rate.

Source: Table 6.4.

CHILDREN'S DEFENSE FUND

Table 6.5

Percent of Adolescent and Young Adult Women in Pregnancy Risk Categories, by Age, 1988 (Percent of All Women in Age Group)

Risk Category	Age 15-19	Age 20-24
Never had intercourse	46.8%	13.6%
No intercourse in past three months	7.7	6.9
Pregnant	2.8	5.5
Postpartum	—	—
Seeking pregnancy	—	4.3
Sterile	1.1	5.0
Using reversible method of contraception	31.6	55.2
Not using contraception	8.6	8.2

—Number too small to calculate a reliable rate.

Source: Jacqueline Darroch Forrest and Susheela Singh, The Sexual and Reproductive Behavior of American Women, 1982-1988, *Family Planning Perspectives*, Vol. 22, No. 5 (September/October 1990), Table 6.

Table 6.6

Trends in Estimated Pregnancy and Abortion Rates Among Women Ages 15 to 19, 1973-1985 (Per 1,000 Women Ages 15 to 19)

Year	Pregnancy Rate	Abortion Rate
1973	96.2	22.8
1974	98.6	26.9
1975	100.9	31.0
1976	101.1	34.3
1977	104.6	37.5
1978	105.4	39.7
1979	109.4	42.4
1980	111.2	42.9
1981	110.8	43.3
1982	110.3	42.9
1983	109.9	43.5
1984	108.6	43.2
1985	109.8	43.8

Source: Stanley K. Henshaw, Asta M. Kenney, Debra Somberg, and Jennifer Van Vort, *Teenage Pregnancy in the United States: The Scope of the Problem and State Responses*, The Alan Guttmacher Institute (1989), Table 5.

Table 6.7

Estimated Pregnancies Among Women Younger than 20, by Age and Outcome of the Pregnancy, 1985

Outcome	Under 15	15-19	15-17	18-19	Under 20
Estimated total pregnancies	30,930	1,000,110	383,540	616,570	1,031,040
Births	10,220	467,485	167,789	299,696	477,705
Legal abortions	16,970	399,200	165,630	233,570	416,170
Estimated miscarriages	3,740	133,420	50,120	83,300	137,160
Estimated percent of pregnancies ending in abortion	54.9%	39.9%	43.2%	37.9%	40.4%

Source: Stanley K. Henshaw, Asta M. Kenney, Debra Somberg, and Jennifer Van Vort, *Teenage Pregnancy in the United States: The Scope of the Problem and State Responses*, The Alan Guttmacher Institute (1989), Table 4.

Table 6.8

Estimated Pregnancy Rates, Estimated Abortion Rates, and Birth Rates Among Women Ages 15 to 19, by Race and Latino Origin, and Age, 1985 (Rates per 1,000 Women Ages 15 to 19)

Outcome, Age	Total	White	Nonwhite	Latina*
Total pregnancies				
Under 15	16.6	8.8	50.8	NA
15-19	109.8	92.9	185.8	158.1
15-17	71.1	57.1	134.0	NA
18-19	166.2	145.1	261.3	NA
Abortion				
Under 15	9.1	5.0	27.0	NA
15-19	43.8	37.8	71.1	50.3
15-17	30.7	25.7	53.2	NA
18-19	63.0	55.4	97.1	NA
Birth				
Under 15	5.5	2.7	17.6	NA
15-19	51.3	42.8	89.7	85.6
15-17	31.1	24.0	62.9	NA
18-19	80.8	70.1	128.7	NA

*Women of Latino origin can be of any race.
NA—Data not available.

Source: Stanley K. Henshaw, Asta M. Kenney, Debra Somberg, and Jennifer Van Vort, *Teenage Pregnancy in the United States: The Scope of the Problem and State Responses*, The Alan Guttmacher Institute (1989), Table 2.

Table 6.9

Trends in Birth Rates Among Adolescent and Young Adult Women, by Race, Marital Status, and Age (Births per 1,000 Women in Specific Category)

Marital Status, Age, Year	Total	White	Black
All marital statuses			
10-14			
1970	1.2	0.5	5.2
1975	1.3	0.6	5.1
1980	1.1	0.6	4.3
1985	1.2	0.6	4.5
1988	1.3	0.6	4.8
15-19			
1970	68.3	57.4	140.7
1975	55.6	46.4	111.8
1980	53.0	44.7	100.0
1985	51.3	42.8	97.4
1988	53.6	43.7	105.9
15-17			
1970	38.8	29.2	101.4
1975	36.1	28.0	85.6
1980	32.5	25.2	73.6
1985	31.1	24.0	69.8
1988	33.8	25.5	76.6
18-19			
1970	114.7	101.5	204.9
1975	85.0	74.0	152.4
1980	82.1	72.1	138.8
1985	80.8	70.1	137.1
1988	81.7	69.2	150.5
20-24			
1970	167.8	163.4	202.7
1975	113.0	108.2	142.8
1980	115.1	109.5	146.3
1985	108.9	102.8	140.8
1988	111.5	102.5	157.5

(Continued on next page)

Table 6.9 *(continued)*

Trends in Birth Rates Among Adolescent and Young Adult Women, by Race, Marital Status, and Age (Births per 1,000 Women in Specific Category)

Marital Status, Age, Year	Total	White	Black
Unmarried			
15-19			
1970	22.4	10.9	96.9
1975	23.9	12.0	93.5
1980	27.6	16.2	89.2
1985	31.6	20.5	88.8
1988	36.8	24.8	98.3
15-17			
1970	17.1	7.5	77.9
1975	19.3	9.6	76.8
1980	20.6	11.8	69.6
1985	22.5	14.2	67.0
1988	26.5	17.1	74.1
18-19			
1970	32.9	17.6	136.4
1975	32.5	16.5	123.8
1980	39.0	23.6	120.2
1985	46.6	30.9	121.1
1988	52.7	36.4	136.1
20-24			
1970	38.4	22.5	131.5
1975	31.2	15.5	108.0
1980	40.9	24.4	115.1
1985	46.8	30.9	116.1
1988	56.7	38.3	138.2

Source: *Monthly Vital Statistics Report*, Vol. 39, No. 4, Supplement, Advance Report of Final Natality Statistics, 1988 (August 15, 1990), Table 4.

Fig. 6.2

Trends in Birth Rates Among Unmarried White Adolescent and Young Adult Women, by Age, 1970-1988

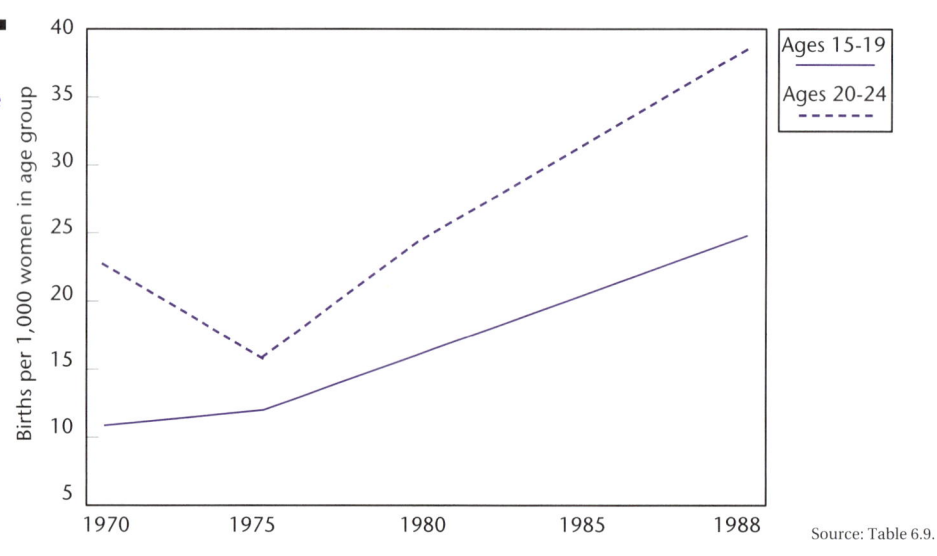

Source: Table 6.9.

Fig. 6.3

Trends in Birth Rates Among Unmarried Black Adolescent and Young Adult Women, by Age, 1970-1988

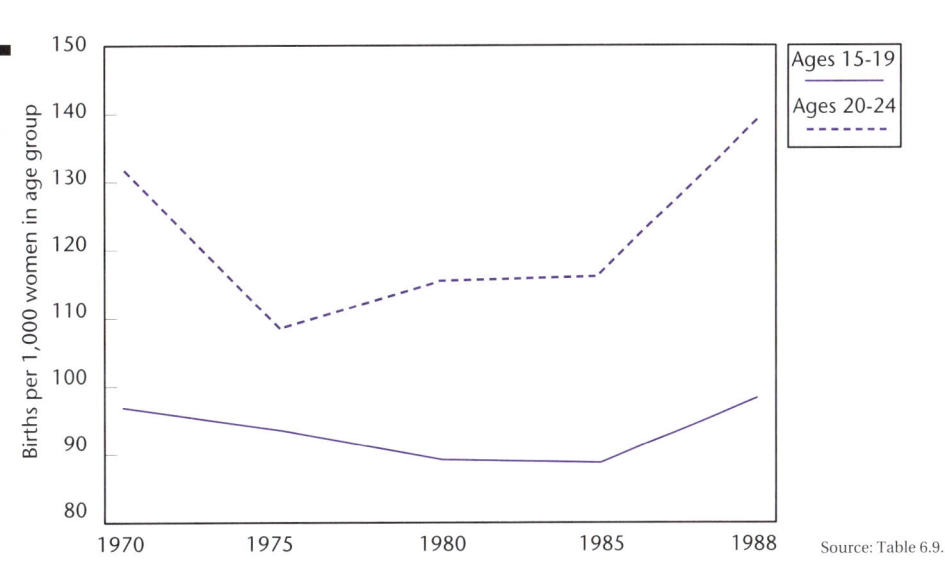

[Line chart showing births per 1,000 women in age group from 1970 to 1988. Ages 15-19 (solid line): approximately 96 in 1970, declining to about 88 in 1980-1985, rising to about 98 in 1988. Ages 20-24 (dashed line): approximately 131 in 1970, dropping to about 108 in 1975, rising gradually to about 116 in 1985, then rising sharply to about 140 in 1988.]

Source: Table 6.9.

Table 6.10

Births to Adolescent and Young Adult Women, by Race and Latino Origin, Marital Status, and Age, 1988

Age	Total	White	Black	Latina*
Total births to teens				
Total under 20	488,941	319,544	152,508	73,858
Under 15	10,588	4,073	6,182	1,621
15-17	176,624	106,907	63,833	28,257
18-19	301,729	208,564	82,493	43,980
20-24	1,067,472	804,622	220,301	143,226
Percent of births that were to unmarried women				
Under 20	65.9%	53.9%	91.5%	59.2%
Under 15	93.6	86.5	98.9	84.9
15-17	77.1	65.9	96.0	68.0
18-19	58.5	47.1	87.4	52.7
20-24	32.9	23.2	68.7	36.2
Teen births as percent of all births	12.5%	10.5%	22.7%	16.4%

*Births to Latina women are based on reports from only 30 reporting states and the District of Columbia; persons of Latino origin can be of any race.

Source: National Center for Health Statistics, *Vital Statistics of the United States: 1988, Vol. I—Natality* (1990), Tables 1-54, 1-76, 1-110, and 1-115. Calculations by Children's Defense Fund.

Table 6.11

Trends in Births to Unmarried Adolescents, 1950-1988

Year	Total Births to Adolescent Women	Births to Unmarried Adolescent Women	Percent of Births to Teens That Were to Unmarried Women
1950	424,556	59,200	13.9%
1960	593,746	68,254	11.5
1970	656,460	199,900	30.5
1980	562,330	271,801	48.3
1988	488,941	322,406	65.9

Source: Public Health Service, *Vital Statistics of the United States: 1950, Volume I* (1954), Table 6.29; Public Health Service, *Vital Statistics of the United States: 1950, Volume II* (1953), Table 21; Public Health Service, *Vital Statistics of the United States: 1960, Volume I—Natality* (1962), Tables 2-12 and 2-22; National Center for Health Statistics, *Vital Statistics of the United States: 1970, Volume I—Natality* (1975), Tables 1-32 and 1-50; National Center for Health Statistics, *Vital Statistics of the United States: 1980, Volume I—Natality* (1984), Tables 1-34 and 1-54; and National Center for Health Statistics, *Vital Statistics of the United States: 1988, Volume I—Natality* (1990), Tables 1-34 and 1-54. Calculations by Children's Defense Fund.

Table 6.12

Births to Date Among Never-Married Women Ages 18 to 29, by Race and Latino Origin, and Age, 1988 (Births Per 1,000 Never-Married Women)

Age	Total	White	Black	Latina*
18-19	100	54	380	27
20-21	189	104	629	387
22-24	309	178	926	587
25-29	570	292	1,447	995

*Women of Latino origin can be of any race.

Source: U.S. Department of Commerce, Bureau of the Census, *Current Population Reports*, Series P-20, No. 436, Fertility of American Women: 1988 (1989), Table 7.

Table 6.13

Percent of Premarital Pregnancies That Resulted in a Marital Birth, by Race and Latino Origin of Woman, and Age, 1970-1988

Age, Year of First Birth	Total	White	Black	Latina*
15-17				
1970-1974	38.4%	53.7%	13.8%	—
1975-1979	26.7	42.5	2.9	18.4%
1980-1984	27.0	34.8	7.7	26.0
1985-1988	17.3	36.6	0.0	—
18-19				
1970-1974	50.7	60.5	28.4	—
1975-1979	46.6	60.3	9.9	—
1980-1984	35.4	44.1	12.4	4.3
1985-1988	27.3	34.6	8.1	—
20-24				
1970-1974	48.9	59.7	14.4	—
1975-1979	42.4	52.9	13.7	38.4
1980-1984	43.5	49.4	22.3	44.2
1985-1988	28.2	39.4	5.2	17.9

*Women of Latino origin can be of any race.
— Number too small to calculate a reliable rate.

Source: U.S. Department of Commerce, Bureau of the Census, *Current Population Reports*, Series P-20, No. 436, Fertility of American Women: 1988 (1989), Table F.

Table 6.14

Women Ages 18 to 24 With Children, by Race and Latino Origin, Marital Status, and Educational Attainment, 1988 (Percent With Children)

Marital Status, Educational Attainment	Total	White	Black	Latina*
All women				
Total	25.8%	22.9%	43.4%	38.1%
Not high school graduate	45.1	43.1	53.5	55.9
High school graduate, no college	30.6	27.4	49.2	34.6
Some college	11.7	9.5	26.5	15.3
College graduate	9.0	7.0	30.6	—
Women never married				
Total	12.5	7.2	37.8	17.8
Not high school graduate	27.9	19.8	48.5	36.4
High school graduate, no college	14.6	8.6	42.7	12.6
Some college	5.3	2.3	22.7	4.0
College graduate	2.0	0.9	—	—

*Women of Latino origin can be of any race.
— Number too small to calculate a reliable rate.

Source: U.S. Department of Commerce, Bureau of the Census, *Current Population Reports*, Series P-20, No. 436, Fertility of American Women: 1988 (1989), Table 2. Calculations by Children's Defense Fund.

Fig. 6.4

Percent of Women Ages 18 to 24 With Children, by Race and Latino Origin, and Educational Attainment, 1988

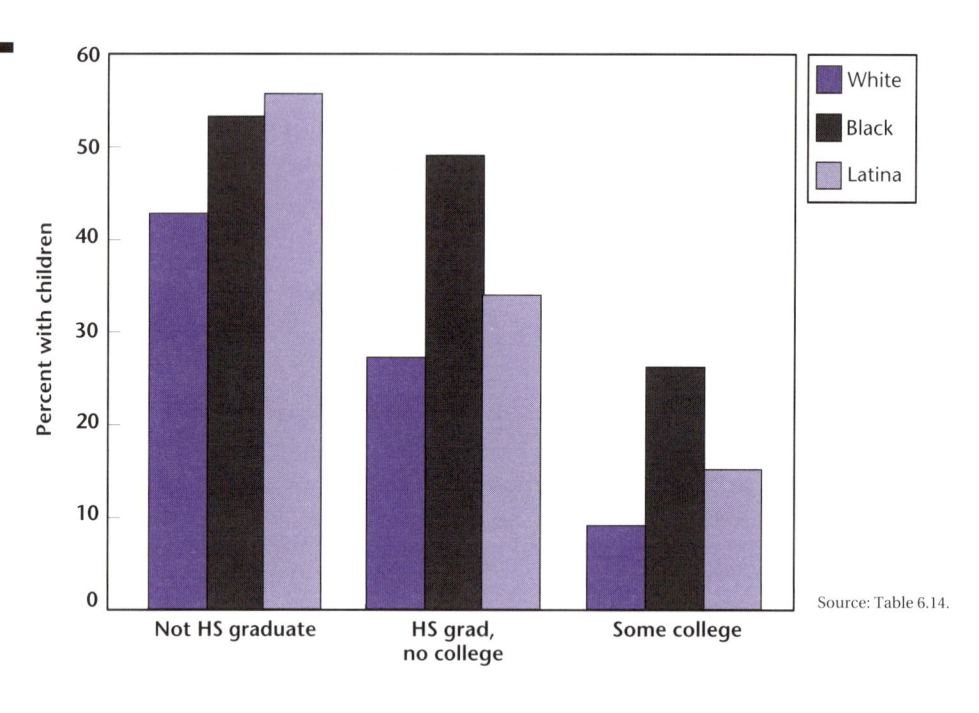

Source: Table 6.14.

Table 6.15

Number of Children Ever Born to Women Ages 18 to 24, by Race and Latino Origin, and by Selected Characteristics, 1988 (Numbers in Thousands)

	Total	White	Black	Latina*
Total number ever born	5,254	3,736	1,362	757
Number ever born to never-married women	1,703	747	922	221
Number ever born to non-high school graduates	1,904	1,369	491	460
Number ever born to never-married, non-high school graduates	717	346	357	160
Number ever born to never-married, non-high school graduates as percent of total ever born	13.6%	9.3%	26.2%	21.1%

*Women of Latino origin can be of any race.

Source: U.S. Department of Commerce, Bureau of the Census, *Current Population Reports*, Series P-20, No. 436, Fertility of American Women: 1988 (1989), Table 2. Calculations by Children's Defense Fund.

Table 6.16

Wanted and Unwanted Childbearing Among Adolescent and Young Adult Mothers, by Race, Marital Status, and Age, 1984-1988 (Percent of Births)

Marital Status, Age, Wantedness of Birth	Total	White	Black
Ever-married, ages 15-24			
Wanted at conception	48.5%	48.9%	48.1%
Wanted but mistimed	42.6	43.4	36.3
Unwanted at conception	8.6	7.4	—
Never-married, ages 15-19			
Wanted at conception	13.3	19.1	10.4
Wanted but mistimed	63.5	70.6	57.5
Unwanted at conception	—	—	—
Never-married, ages 20-24			
Wanted at conception	31.3	34.1	26.2
Wanted but mistimed	42.6	49.5	36.3
Unwanted at conception	26.1	16.5	37.5

— Number too small to calculate a reliable rate.

Source: National Center for Health Statistics, *Advance Data*, Number 189, Wanted and Unwanted Childbearing in the United States: 1973-1988, Data from the National Survey of Family Growth (September 26, 1990), Tables 1 and 4. Calculations by Children's Defense Fund.

Table 6.17

Trends in Marriage Among Adolescents and Young Adults, by Gender and Age, 1890-1989 (Percent Ever Married)

Age, Year	Men	Women
15-19		
1890	0.6%	9.7%
1900	1.2	11.3
1910	1.7	12.1
1920	2.3	13.0
1930	2.0	13.2
1940	1.7	11.9
1950	3.3	17.1
1960	3.9	16.1
1970	4.1	11.9
1980	2.8	8.8
1989	1.2	4.8
20-24		
1890	19.3	48.2
1900	22.4	48.4
1910	25.1	51.7
1920	29.3	54.4
1930	29.2	54.0
1940	27.8	52.8
1950	40.9	67.7
1960	46.9	71.6
1970	45.3	64.2
1980	31.2	49.8
1989	22.6	37.5

Source: U.S. Department of Commerce, Bureau of the Census, *Census of Population: 1960, Volume I, Part 1* (1961), Table 177; U.S. Department of Commerce, Bureau of the Census, *1970 Census of Population, Volume I, Chapter D, Part 1* (1973), Table 203; U.S. Department of Commerce, Bureau of the Census, *1980 Census of Population, Volume I, Chapter D, Part 1* (1984), Table 264; and U.S. Department of Commerce, Bureau of the Census, *Current Population Reports*, Series P-20, No. 445, Marital Status and Living Arrangements: March 1989 (1990), Tables B and 1. Calculations by Children's Defense Fund.

Fig. 6.5

Trends in Marriage Among 20- to 24-Year-Olds, by Gender, 1890-1989

Source: Table 6.17.

Table 6.18

Trends in Median Age at First Marriage, by Gender, 1890-1989

Year	Men	Women
1890	26.1	22.0
1900	25.9	21.9
1910	25.1	21.6
1920	24.6	21.2
1930	24.3	21.3
1940	24.3	21.5
1950	22.8	20.3
1960	22.8	20.3
1970	23.2	20.8
1980	24.7	22.0
1989	26.2	23.8

Source: U.S. Department of Commerce, Bureau of the Census, *Current Population Reports*, Series P-20, No. 445, Marital Status and Living Arrangements: March 1989 (1990), Table A.

Table 6.19

Trends in Marriage, by Race and Latino Origin, Gender, and Age, 1970-1989 (Percent Ever Married)

Gender, Age, Year	Total	White	Black	Latino*
Male				
15-19				
1970	NA	NA	NA	NA
1980	2.7	3.0	1.2	4.2
1989	1.2	1.3	0.8	3.3
20-24				
1970	44.8	45.5	40.6	NA
1980	31.4	33.1	21.0	40.1
1989	22.6	24.0	15.1	32.0
Female				
15-19				
1970	NA	NA	NA	NA
1980	8.9	9.6	4.6	11.8
1989	4.8	5.5	1.8	11.5
20-24				
1970	64.1	65.3	56.7	NA
1980	49.8	52.8	31.3	57.1
1989	37.5	40.1	22.1	50.3

*Persons of Latino origin can be of any race.

NA—Data not available.

Source: U.S. Department of Commerce, Bureau of the Census, *Current Population Reports*, Series P-20, No. 212, Marital Status and Family Status (1971), Table 1; U.S. Department of Commerce, Bureau of the Census, *Current Population Reports*, Series P-20, No. 365, Marital Status and Living Arrangements: March 1980 (1981), Table 1; and U.S. Department of Commerce, Bureau of the Census, *Current Population Reports*, Series P-20, No. 445, Marital Status and Living Arrangements: March 1989 (1990), Table 1. Calculations by Children's Defense Fund.

Table 6.20

Ratio of Males to Females, by Race and Latino Origin, and Age, 1989 (Males Per 100 Females)

Age	Total	White	Black	Latino*
Under 10	104.8	105.3	103.3	104.0
10-14	105.2	105.6	103.3	104.0
15-19	104.6	104.7	102.6	104.5
20-24	101.8	102.7	95.4	108.0
25-29	101.2	102.8	91.8	113.0
30-39	99.9	101.9	87.7	107.2
40-49	96.2	98.3	82.4	95.3
50-59	92.7	94.3	81.7	90.1

*Persons of Latino origin can be of any race.

Source: U.S. Department of Commerce, Bureau of the Census, *Current Population Reports*, Series P-25, No. 1057, U.S. Population Estimates, by Age, Sex, Race, and Hispanic Origin: 1989 (1990), Table 1. Calculations by Children's Defense Fund.

Table 6.21

Cohabitation and Marriage Among Adolescent and Young Adult Women, by Race and Age, 1988 (Percent)

Cohabitation/Marriage Status, Age	Total	White	Black
Ever cohabited			
15-19	8.4%	9.3%	—
20-24	32.4	34.2	29.0%
Ever married			
15-19	3.7	4.4	—
20-24	38.6	42.9	23.6
Cohabited before first marriage			
15-19	8.2	9.2	—
20-24	30.3	31.6	28.6

— Number too small to calculate a reliable rate.

Source: National Center for Health Statistics, *Advance Data*, Number 194, Cohabitation, Marriage, Marital Dissolution, and Remarriage: United States, 1988, Data from the National Survey of Family Growth (January 4, 1991), Table 1.

Listing of Tables and Figures

Tables

Table 1.1 Trends in the Adolescent and Young Adult Population, by Race and Latino Origin, 1970-2030 46

Table 1.2 Trends in the Ratio of Adolescents and Young Adults to Senior Citizens, 1970-2030 46

Table 1.3 Adolescent and Young Adult Population, by Race and Age, 1989..47

Table 1.4 Latino Adolescent and Young Adult Population, by Latino Subgroup and Age, 1989 47

Table 1.5 Adolescent and Young Adult Population, Races Other Than Black and White, by Race and Age, 1980 48

Table 1.6 Regional Distribution of School-Age Children and Young Adults, by Race and Latino Origin and by Age, 1990 49

Table 1.7 Residential Distribution of Families with Adolescents Ages 12 to 17, by Race and Latino Origin and Family Type, 1989......................................49

Table 1.8 Living Arrangements of Adolescents Ages 10 to 17, by Race and Latino Origin and Age, 1989 50

Table 1.9 Trends in Percent of Adolescents Ages 10 to 17 Living With One Parent Only, by Race and Latino Origin, 1970-1989 51

Table 1.10 Trends in the Poverty Rate Among School-Age Children and Young Adults, by Race and Latino Origin and by Age, 1969-1989 52

Table 1.11 Distribution of Family Income Among Families with Adolescents Ages 12 to 17, by Race and Latino Origin, 1989 52

Table 1.12 Adolescents Ages 12 to 17, by Race and Latino Origin, Family Type, and Age of Parent, 1989..53

Table 1.13 Adolescents Ages 12 to 17, by Race and Latino Origin, Family Type, and Education of Parent, 1989 53

Table 1.14 Adolescents Ages 12 to 17, by Race and Latino Origin, Family Type, and Parental Employment Status, 1989...54

Table 1.15 Housing Arrangements of Families With Adolescents Ages 12 to 17, by Race and Latino Origin and Family Type, 1989 55

Table 1.16 Trends in Percent of Adolescents Living in Doubled-Up Families, by Race and Latino Origin and Family Type, 1970-1988 55

Table 2.1 Perceived Health Status by Race and Latino Origin, Age, Gender, and Poverty Status, 1988 60

Table 2.2 Rates for Selected Notifiable Diseases Among Adolescents and Young Adults, by Age, 1989 61

Table 2.3 Trends in Rates for Selected Notifiable Diseases, 1950-1989   61

Table 2.4 Prevalence of Disability Among Adolescents and Young Adults, by Age and Various Characteristics, 1984 62

Table 2.5 Leading Causes of Disability Among Adolescents and Young Adults, by Age, 1984...62

Table 2.6 Trends in Adolescent and Young Adult Death Rates, by Selected Causes and Age, 1960-1988 63

Table 2.7 Leading Causes of Death Among Adolescents and Young Adults, Ages 15 to 24, 1988 64

Table 2.8 Firearm Death Rates Among Adolescents and Young Adults, by Race, Gender, and Age, 1988 64

Table 2.9 Homicide Death Rates Among Adolescents and Young Adults, by Race, Gender, and Age, 1988..66

Table 2.10 Suicide Death Rates Among Adolescents and Young Adults, by Race, Gender, and Age, 1988 66

THE ADOLESCENT AND YOUNG ADULT FACT BOOK

Table 2.11 Accident Death Rates Among Adolescents and Young Adults, by Race, Gender, and Age, 1988..**67**

Table 2.12 Motor Vehicle Accident Death Rates Among Adolescents and Young Adults, by Race, Gender, and Age, 1988 ....**68**

Table 2.13 Recency of Physician Visit, by Race and Latino Origin, Age, and Poverty Status, 1988 ....**69**

Table 2.14 Recency of Dental Visit, by Race and Latino Origin, Age, and Poverty Status, 1986 ....**69**

Table 2.15 Adolescents Not Receiving Routine Health Care, by Race and Latino Origin and by Age, 1988 ....**70**

Table 2.16 Adolescents With No Regular Source of Health Care, by Race and Latino Origin and by Age, 1988...**70**

Table 2.17 Health Insurance Coverage of Adolescents and Young Adults, by Age and Various Characteristics, 1984..**71**

Table 2.18 Health Insurance Coverage of Adolescents and Young Adults, by Age and Perceived Health Status, 1984..**71**

Table 2.19 Health Insurance Coverage of Adolescents and Young Adults, by Race and Latino Origin and by Age, 1988...**72**

Table 3.1 Trends in the Use of Illicit Drugs Among Adolescents and Young Adults, by Gender and Age, 1985-1990 ....**77**

Table 3.2 Marijuana Use by Adolescents and Young Adults, by Race and Latino Origin, Gender, and Age, 1988..**77**

Table 3.3 Cocaine Use by Adolescents and Young Adults, by Race and Latino Origin, Gender, and Age, 1988..**78**

Table 3.4 Crack Use by Adolescents and Young Adults, by Race and Latino Origin, and Age, 1988 ....**79**

Table 3.5 Alcohol Use by Adolescents and Young Adults, by Race and Latino Origin, Gender, and Age, 1988..**79**

Table 3.6 Heavy Alcohol Use by Adolescents and Young Adults, by Race and Latino Origin, and Age, 1988..**80**

Table 3.7 Cigarette Use by Adolescents and Young Adults, by Race and Latino Origin, Gender, and Age, 1988..**81**

Table 3.8 Current Drug, Alcohol, and Cigarette Use Among Adolescents and Young Adults, by Specific Substance and Age, 1988..................................**81**

Table 3.9 Types of Substances Used by Adolescents and Young Adults, by Age and by Substance, 1988 ....**82**

Table 3.10 Average Age At First Use of Cigarettes, Alcohol, and Other Drugs, by Current Age, 1988 ....**82**

Table 3.11 Drug and Alcohol Use by High School Seniors, by College Plans, 1990 ....**83**

Table 3.12 Trends in Daily Marijuana and Alcohol Use and in Binge Drinking Among High School Seniors, 1975-1990 ....**83**

Table 3.13 Trends in Arrest Rates Among 18-Year-Olds, by Gender and Type of Crime, 1965-1988 ....**85**

Table 3.14 Trends in Arrest Rates for Drunk Driving Among 18- to 24-Year-Olds, 1976-1986...**85**

Table 3.15 Committed Juvenile Offenders, by Race and Latino Origin and by Age, 1987 ....**86**

Table 3.16 Primary Childhood Living Arrangements of Committed Juvenile Offenders, by Race and Latino Origin and by Age, 1987...................**86**

Table 3.17 Alcohol and Drug Histories of Committed Juvenile Offenders, by Age, 1987 ....**87**

Table 3.18 Characteristics of Children in Custody, by Public or Private Status of the Facility, February 1, 1985 and February 15, 1989.......................**87**

Table 3.19 Juveniles Held in Public and Private Juvenile Facilities, by Gender and by Reason Held, February 1, 1985...**88**

Table 3.20 Criminal Victimization Among Adolescents and Young Adults, by Race, Type of Crime, Gender, and Age, 1988 ....**89**

Table 3.21 Average Annual Rate of Handgun Crime Victimization, by Race, Gender, and Age, 1979-1987 90

Table 4.1 Trends in School Enrollment, by Age, Level, and Gender, 1960-1988 97
Table 4.2 School Enrollment, by Race and Latino Origin, Level, Gender, and Age, 1988 98
Table 4.3 Trends in School Enrollment, by Race and Latino Origin, Level, and Age, 1970-1988 99
Table 4.4 Students Behind in School, by Gender, Age, and Race and Latino Origin, 1988 100
Table 4.5 Special Education Placements, by Race and Latino Origin, 1986 101
Table 4.6 Trends in School Desegregation for Black and Latino Children, 1968-1986 101
Table 4.7 Math and Science Course-Taking Patterns, by Race and Latino Origin, 1987 High School Graduates 102
Table 4.8 Suspension and Corporal Punishment, by Race and Latino Origin, 1986 103
Table 4.9 Students At or Above Different Proficiency Levels, by Subject and Age, 1986 and 1988 104
Table 4.10 Students At or Above Expected Level of Proficiency, by Gender, Age, and Subject, 1986 and 1988 104
Table 4.11 Average Achievement Scores, by Race and Latino Origin, Subject, and Age, 1986-1988 105
Table 4.12 Student Achievement At or Above Expected Level of Proficiency, by Age, and Race and Latino Origin 105
Table 4.13 Student Reading and Math Achievement, by Age and Parents' Education, 1986 and 1988 107
Table 4.14 Average SAT Scores, by Racial and Ethnic Group, 1990 108
Table 4.15 Trends in Enrollment and Educational Attainment of 18- to 24-Year-Olds, by Race and Latino Origin, 1967-1988 108
Table 4.16 Years of School Completed Among 20- to 24-Year-Olds, by Race and Latino Origin, 1988 109
Table 4.17 Trends in Dropout Rates, by Race and Latino Origin, and by Age, 1970-1988 110
Table 4.18 School Completion Status, by Race and Latino Origin, and Age, 1988 111
Table 4.19 School Enrollment and Educational Attainment Among 20- and 21-Year-Olds, by Race and Poverty Status, 1987 112
Table 4.20 Dropout Rates Among 16- to 24-Year-Olds, by Race and Latino Origin, and by Metropolitan Status, 1988 112
Table 4.21 College Attainment Among 18- to 21-Year-Old High School Graduates, by Race and Poverty Status, 1975 and 1987 113
Table 4.22 Trends in Highest Degree Attained Four Years After High School, by Race and Latino Origin and by Socioeconomic Status, 1972-1982 113
Table 4.23 Trends in Postsecondary Attainment Four Years After High School, by Type of High School and by Academic Program, 1972-1982 114

Table 5.1 Trends in the Employment-Population Ratio of Adolescents and Young Adults, by Race and Latino Origin, Age, and Gender, 1973-1989 118
Table 5.2 Trends in the Unemployment Rate of Adolescents and Young Adults, by Race and Latino Origin, Age, and Gender, 1973-1989 119
Table 5.3 Employment Status of Adolescents and Young Adults, by Race and Latino Origin, School Enrollment Status, and Age, 1989 120
Table 5.4 Employment Status of Adolescents and Young Adults Ages 16 to 24 Not Enrolled in School, by Race and Latino Origin and Educational Attainment, 1989 120

Table 5.5 Full-Time Employment Status of Adolescents and Young Adults, by Race, Gender, and Age, 1989 121

Table 5.6 Reasons for Working Part Time Among Adolescents and Young Adults, by Race, Age, and Gender, 1989..122

Table 5.7 Percent of Population on Active Military Duty, by Race, Gender, and Age, June 1988 123

Table 5.8 Median Weekly Earnings of 16- to 24-Year-Old Full-Time Wage and Salary Workers, by Race and Latino Origin and by Gender, 1979-1989 123

Table 5.9 Median Weekly Earnings of Full-Time Workers Ages 16 to 24 as a Percent of Earnings of Full-Time Workers Ages 25 and Older, by Race and Latino Origin and by Gender, 1979-1989 124

Table 5.10 Annual Earnings of Young Adults Ages 18 to 24, by Race and Latino Origin, Employment Status, Gender, and Educational Attainment, 1987 124

Table 5.11 Annual Income of Young Adults Ages 18 to 24 Who Work Full Time, Year-Round, by Race and Latino Origin, Gender, and Marital Status, 1987 125

Table 5.12 Sources of Income Among Youths Ages 15 to 24, by Gender, 1987 125

Table 5.13 Adolescent and Young Adult AFDC Recipients, by Gender, AFDC Status, and Age, 1988 126

Table 6.1 Trends in Sexual Initiation Among Unmarried Women Ages 15 to 19, 1970-1988 131

Table 6.2 Age of Initiation of Sexual Intercourse, by Race and Latino Origin and Gender, and Age of Women At First Pregnancy, 1983-1984 131

Table 6.3 Sexual Activity Among Women Ages 15 to 19, by Race and Latino Origin, and by Age, 1988 132

Table 6.4 Contraceptive Use At First Intercourse Among Women Ages 15 to 19, by Race and Latino Origin, and by Method Used, 1988 132

Table 6.5 Percent of Adolescent and Young Adult Women in Pregnancy Risk Categories, by Age, 1988 133

Table 6.6 Trends in Estimated Pregnancy and Abortion Rates Among Women Ages 15 to 19, 1973-1985 133

Table 6.7 Estimated Pregnancies Among Women Younger than 20, by Age and Outcome of the Pregnancy, 1985 134

Table 6.8 Estimated Pregnancy Rates, Estimated Abortion Rates, and Birth Rates Among Women Ages 15 to 19, by Race and Latino Origin, and Age, 1985 134

Table 6.9 Trends in Birth Rates Among Adolescent and Young Adult Women, by Race, Marital Status, and Age 135

Table 6.10 Births to Adolescent and Young Adult Women, by Race and Latino Origin, Marital Status, and Age, 1988...137

Table 6.11 Trends in Births to Unmarried Adolescents, 1950-1988 138

Table 6.12 Births to Date Among Never-Married Women Ages 18 to 29, by Race and Latino Origin, and Age, 1988 138

Table 6.13 Percent of Premarital Pregnancies that Resulted in a Marital Birth, by Race and Latino Origin of Woman, and Age, 1970-1988 139

Table 6.14 Women Ages 18 to 24 With Children, by Race and Latino Origin, Marital Status, and Educational Attainment, 1988 139

Table 6.15 Number of Children Ever Born to Women Ages 18 to 24, by Race and Latino Origin, and by Selected Characteristics, 1988 140

Table 6.16 Wanted and Unwanted Childbearing Among Adolescent and Young Adult Mothers, by Race, Marital Status, and Age, 1984-1988 141

Table 6.17 Trends in Marriage Among Adolescents and Young Adults, by Gender and Age, 1890-1989 141

Table 6.18 Trends in Median Age at First Marriage, by Gender, 1890-1989..142

Table 6.19 Trends in Marriage, by Race and Latino Origin, Gender, and Age, 1970–1989 143
Table 6.20 Ratio of Males to Females, by Race and Latino Origin, and Age, 1989 144
Table 6.21 Cohabitation and Marriage Among Adolescent and Young Adult Women, by Race and Age, 1988 144

Figures

Figure 1.1 Adolescents and Young Adults Ages 10 to 24 as a Percent of the Population, by Race and Latino Subgroup, 1989 48
Figure 1.2 Percent of Families with Adolescents Ages 12 to 17 Living in Central Cities, by Family Type and Race and Latino Origin, 1989 50
Figure 1.3 Trends in Percent of Adolescents Ages 10 to 17 Living with One Parent Only, by Race and Latino Origin, 1970-1989 51
Figure 1.4 Percent of Adolescents Ages 12 to 17 Whose Parent Is Not a High School Graduate, by Family Type and Race and Latino Origin, 1989 54

Figure 2.1 Perceived Health Status of School-Age Children and Young Adults, by Age, Gender, and Poverty Status, 1988 60
Figure 2.2 Firearm Death Rates Among Adolescent and Young Adult Males, by Age and Race, 1988 65
Figure 2.3 Homicide Death Rates Among Adolescent and Young Adult Males, by Age and Race, 1988 65
Figure 2.4 Suicide Death Rates Among Adolescents and Young Adults, by Age, Race, and Gender, 1988 67
Figure 2.5 Motor Vehicle Accident Death Rates Among Adolescents and Young Adults, by Race, Gender, and Age, 1988 68
Figure 2.6 Health Insurance Status of Adolescents, by Race and Latino Origin, 1988 72

Figure 3.1 Current Marijuana Use by Adolescents and Young Adults, by Race and Latino Origin, Gender, and Age, 1988 78
Figure 3.2 Current Alcohol Use by Adolescents and Young Adults, by Race and Latino Origin, Gender, and Age, 1988 80
Figure 3.3 Trends in Daily Marijuana and Alcohol Use Among High School Seniors, 1975-1990 84
Figure 3.4 Trends in Binge Drinking Among High School Seniors, 1975-1990 84
Figure 3.5 Criminal Victimization Among Adolescents and Young Adults, by Race, Gender, and Age, Violent Crimes, 1988 90
Figure 3.6 Handgun Crime Victimization Among Adolescents and Young Adults, by Race, Gender, and Age, Annual Average, 1979-1987 91

Figure 4.1 Adolescents Behind in School, by Race and Latino Origin, Age, and Gender, 1988 100
Figure 4.2 School Desegregation for Black and Latino Children, 1968 and 1986 102
Figure 4.3 High School Graduates Who Took Selected Math Courses, by Race and Latino Origin, 1987 103
Figure 4.4 Students Reading At or Above Expected Level of Proficiency, by Race and Latino Origin and by Age, 1988 106
Figure 4.5 Years of School Completed by 20- to 24-Year-Olds, by Race and Latino Origin, 1988 109
Figure 4.6 High School Graduation Rates, by Race and Latino Origin and Age, 1988 111

Figure 5.1 The Employment–Population Ratio of Adolescents and Young Adults, by Age, Race and Latino Origin, and Gender, 1989 ....**118**

Figure 5.2 The Unemployment Rate of Adolescents and Young Adults, by Age, Race and Latino Origin, and Gender, 1989 ....**119**

Figure 5.3 Employment–Population Ratio of Youths Ages 16 to 24 Not Enrolled in School, by Race and Latino Origin and Educational Attainment, 1989 ....**121**

Figure 6.1 Contraceptive Use At First Intercourse Among Women Ages 15 to 19, by Race and Latino Origin, and by Method Used, 1988 ....**132**

Figure 6.2 Trends in Birth Rates Among Unmarried White Adolescent and Young Adult Women, by Age, 1970-1988 ....**136**

Figure 6.3 Trends in Birth Rates Among Unmarried Black Adolescent and Young Adult Women, by Age, 1970-1988 ....**137**

Figure 6.4 Percent of Women Ages 18 to 24 With Children, by Race and Latino Origin, and Educational Attainment, 1988 ....**140**

Figure 6.5 Trends in Marriage Among 20- to 24-Year-Olds, by Gender, 1890-1989 ....**142**

CDF's Child, Youth, and Family Futures Clearinghouse

The following reports are also available from the Children's Defense Fund ($4.50 each, except the January/March 1988 and January/March 1990 double issues, $7.45 each). A complete library of the 30-report Clearinghouse series is available for $85 (35% off the single-issue price). All report prices include postage.

The Health of America's Children (May 1991)

Child Poverty in America (March 1991)

Homeless Families: Failed Policies and Young Victims (Jan. 1991)

Building Youth Corps (Nov. 1990)

An Advocate's Guide to Improving Education (Sept. 1990)

Improving Health Programs for Low-Income Youths (July 1990)

An Advocate's Guide to Fund Raising (May 1990)

Latino Youths at a Crossroads (Jan./March 1990 double issue, $7.45)

Where To Find Data About Adolescents and Youths: A Guide to Sources (Nov. 1989)

Evaluating Your Adolescent Pregnancy Program: How To Get Started (Sept. 1989)

Lack of Health Insurance Makes a Difference (July 1989)

Service Opportunities for Youths (May 1989)

Tackling the Youth Employment Problem (March 1989)

Lessons of Multi-Site Initiatives Serving High-Risk Youths (Jan. 1989)

Teens and AIDS: Opportunities for Prevention (Nov. 1988)

Making the Middle Grades Work (Sept. 1988)

What About the Boys? Teenage Pregnancy Prevention Strategies (July 1988)

Adolescent and Young Adult Fathers: Problems and Solutions (May 1988)

Teenage Pregnancy: An Advocate's Guide to the Numbers (Jan./March 1988 double issue, $7.45)

Child Support and Teen Parents (Nov. 1987)

Teens in Foster Care: Preventing Pregnancy and Building Self-Sufficiency (Sept. 1987)

Opportunities for Prevention: Building After-School and Summer Programs for Young Adolescents (July 1987)

Declining Earnings of Young Men: Their Relation to Poverty, Teen Pregnancy, and Family Formation (May 1987)

Child Care: An Essential Service for Teen Parents (March 1987)

Adolescent Pregnancy: An Anatomy of a Social Problem in Search of Comprehensive Solutions (Jan. 1987)

Welfare and Teen Pregnancy: What Do We Know? What Do We Do? (Nov. 1986)

Preventing Adolescent Pregnancy: What Schools Can Do (Sept. 1986)

Model Programs: Preventing Adolescent Pregnancy and Building Youth Self-Sufficiency (July 1986)

Building Health Programs for Teenagers (May 1986)

Adolescent Pregnancy: What the States Are Saying (March 1986)

Adolescent Pregnancy: Whose Problem Is It? (Jan. 1986)

Order reports from CDF Publications, 122 C Street, N.W., Washington, DC 20001, (202) 628-8787. Orders under $25 must be accompanied by payment.